THE AI PLANET UNVEILED! TRANSCENDING MACHINE CODE, A DEFINITIVE AI GUIDE

EASY GUIDE TO UNDERSTAND ARTIFICIAL INTELLIGENCE: BASICS FROM BEGINNERS TO ADVANCED CONCEPTS, GENERATIVE AI, PYTHON, AND MORE

EARL M. DARWING

CONTENTS

INTRODUCTION

> *I imagine a world in which AI is going to make us work more productively, live longer, and have cleaner energy.*
>
> — FEI-FEI LI

As we stand at the edge of a transformative era, Artificial Intelligence (AI) emerges not just as a technological marvel but as a catalyst poised to redefine our world. It's a journey into a realm where AI extends beyond being a mere tool—it becomes a companion that promises to enhance our productivity, ensure our well-being, and steward the environment towards sustainability.

The heart of AI's transformation lies in its unparalleled ability to innovate; It's not merely about automating tasks but about opening doors to once unreachable possibilities. Imagine AI as a partner in our collective quest for a brighter, more efficient future. AI is already making waves, from revolutionizing our communication with tools like ChatGPT, sparking creativity with DALL-E 3's visual masterpieces, and aiding innovation with Midjourney's design concepts.

But AI's impact extends far beyond these well-known applications. AI's true versatility shines in the less heralded yet equally vital uses. Consider AlertCalifornia's early wildfire detection, Alitheon's authentication of objects, TrailGuard AI's protection of endangered species, Dedrone's security measures against illegal drones, and Audioshake's breakthroughs in music production. These examples underscore the transformative potential of AI across various sectors.

However, despite AI's vast potential, barriers exist that prevent many from fully embracing this technology. Misconceptions about AI's complexity, psychological barriers, and a lack of accessible resources stand in the way, leading to missed opportunities for personal and societal advancement.

This book is your bridge over these barriers. Tailored to demystify AI and make it accessible, it aims to empower you with the knowledge and confidence needed to navigate the AI landscape, whether you're a newcomer or a seasoned professional seeking to deepen your understanding.

Embarking on this journey with AI offers a host of benefits:

- **Unlock the Power of AI**: Discover innovative ways to use AI in your daily life, enhancing both personal and professional aspects.

- **Navigate AI with Confidence**: Gain comprehensive insights into AI's ethical, societal, and technological facets, equipping you to make informed decisions.
- **Stay Ahead of the Curve**: As AI continues to evolve, this book lays the foundation for lifelong learning, ensuring you remain at the forefront of this dynamic field.

By exploring the pages of this book, you'll find that AI is not a force to fear but a tool to wield—a means to amplify our capabilities and enrich our lives. It's about perceiving AI as an ally in our quest to solve complex challenges, improve efficiency, and uncover new opportunities.

As we delve deeper, we touch on AI's history and origins, drawing parallels between the marvels of the human brain and AI's attempts to replicate cognitive processes. This exploration serves as a testament to the profound connection between human intelligence and artificial ingenuity, highlighting the intricate dance between the elegance of the human brain and the precision of artificial neural networks.

This journey through AI is just beginning, and the landscape of possibilities is vast and uncharted. With the insights gained from this book, you're equipped to embrace AI as a valuable partner in crafting a better future.

So, let's embark on this adventure with enthusiasm and an open mind, ready to unlock the potential that AI holds. Remember, your curiosity and willingness to explore the world of AI are commendable steps toward a future filled with endless possibilities. Let's dive in, learn together, and envision a world where AI not only solves our most complex problems but also enhances our daily lives in unimaginable ways.

In this journey, AI is not just a subject to be studied but a revolution to be part of—a transformative force that beckons us to explore, understand, and harness its potential. This book is not just a guide; it's a companion on your journey into the heart of AI, designed to transform curiosity into knowledge and apprehension into mastery.

Together, we embark on an exciting journey, one that promises to expand your horizons and empower you with a deeper understanding of AI. With each page turned you're not only learning about AI but also stepping closer to a future where AI is an integral part of our lives, enhancing our world in ways we've only begun to imagine.

1

THE MARVEL OF THE HUMAN BRAIN AND AI ORIGINS

> *And nowadays, the idea of AI is not really science fiction anymore - it's just science fact.*
>
> — LISA JOY

This profound observation underscores a transformative journey from the annals of speculative fiction into the tangible reality of today's technological landscape. At the heart of this odyssey lies an enduring fascination with the human brain—a marvel of nature that has inspired generations of scientists, philosophers, and technologists to dream of creating intelligence that mirrors our own.

The quest to understand the brain's intricate architecture and its unparalleled processing capabilities has propelled us into the era of AI, a field that promises to redefine the boundaries of possibility. This chapter embarks on a journey to explore the symbiotic relationship between the marvels of the human brain and the origins of AI, setting the stage for a comprehensive exploration of AI's evolution and its profound impact on the world.

UNDERSTANDING THE HUMAN BRAIN: A SYMPHONY OF COMPLEXITY

The human brain, often likened to the most sophisticated computer ever known, is a marvel of biological engineering. It orchestrates a symphony of functions that define our thoughts, emotions, actions, and interactions. This complex organ, with its billions of neurons and trillions of synapses, serves as the blueprint for the digital cosmos of AI.

At the core of the brain's functionality are its distinct regions, each contributing to the tapestry of human cognition and emotion. The frontal lobe, responsible for decision-making and emotional regulation, mirrors the AI algorithms' capacity for complex problem-solving and adaptability. Similarly, the temporal lobe's role in processing auditory information and encoding memories finds its counterpart in AI's ability to learn from data and improve over time (Hines, 2018).

The exploration of the brain's architecture not only enriches our appreciation for its intricacies but also sheds light on the profound inspiration it provides for the evolving field of artificial intelligence. As we delve deeper into understanding how each part of the brain plays a role in the grand symphony of our thoughts and emotions, we uncover parallels with AI's attempts to replicate these processes through neural networks and machine learning.

Neural Networks: Bridging Biology and Technology

The development of artificial neural networks represents a major achievement in replicating the brain's processing abilities. Inspired by the brain's structure, neural networks comprise layers of interconnected nodes that simulate the function of biological neurons. This architecture enables AI systems to recognize patterns, make predictions, and learn from experience, mirroring the brain's ability to adapt and evolve based on sensory input and feedback (*What Is a Neural Network? AI and ML Guide*, n.d.).

The parallels between neural networks and brain functionality highlight the brain-inspired approach to AI development. By examining how neurons communicate through synapses, AI researchers have developed algorithms that mimic these biological processes, enabling machines to process information and make decisions in ways that resemble human cognition (IBM Data and AI Team, 2023).

The brain's complexity has not only inspired the development of neural networks but has also guided the broader trajectory of AI research. The Brain-Inspired Approach to AI seeks to replicate the adaptability and efficiency of the human mind, aiming to create systems that can learn, reason, and interact with the environment in increasingly sophisticated ways. This approach acknowledges the brain as the ultimate model of computational power and versatility, driving efforts to develop AI that can match or even surpass human intelligence in certain tasks (Choi, 2023).

SO, WHAT IS AI?

Artificial Intelligence, in its essence, is the pursuit of creating machines capable of performing tasks that typically require human intelligence. This includes learning from experience, understanding complex content, making decisions based on incomplete information, and recognizing patterns in vast datasets. AI stands as a testament to human ingenuity, extending far beyond the realm of sophisticated machines into the profound depths of learning and adaptation (Burns, 2022).

AI's significance in today's world is undeniable, revolutionizing sectors as diverse as healthcare, finance, education, and entertainment. By harnessing the power of AI, we unlock new possibilities for innovation, efficiency, and problem-solving, reflecting the ever-evolving nature of this dynamic field.

As we delve into the foundations of AI, we embark on an enlightening journey to understand the essence of intelligence—both biological and artificial. This exploration not only celebrates the marvels of the human brain but also sets the stage for a deeper appreciation of AI's potential to transform our world. In the chapters that follow, we will navigate the history, theories, and applications of AI, building upon the foundational understanding established in this chapter.

In this journey of discovery, each insight into the human brain and the origins of AI serves as a stepping stone toward unraveling the mysteries of intelligence. The marvel of the human brain, with its intricate design and profound capabilities, remains the beacon of inspiration guiding our exploration of AI. As we venture forward, we carry with us a spirit of curiosity and a vision of a future where the synergy between humans and AI unlocks new horizons of potential.

Early AI Concepts and Theories

The origins of AI can be traced back to a blend of mythology, philosophy, and early scientific thought long before the term "artificial intelligence" was coined. However, it was during the 20th century that AI began to take shape as a distinct field of study, propelled by the convergence of various scientific disciplines and the advent of computing technology.

One of the earliest figures to conceptualize the idea of machines capable of performing tasks reserved for human intelligence was the British polymath Ada Lovelace. In the mid-19th century, Lovelace speculated that machines might one day "manipulate symbols" to execute tasks beyond mere calculation, hinting at the foundational concept of AI (Zwolak, 2023).

However, it was Alan Turing, a British mathematician and logician, who significantly advanced the conceptual framework for AI. Turing's work proposed the idea that machines could be designed to mimic human thought processes. He introduced the Turing Test as a criterion for determining a machine's capability to exhibit intelligent behavior indistinguishable from that of a human, laying a philosophical and practical foundation for AI research (Copeland, 2019).

Perceptrons, Cybernetics, and the Evolutionary Path of AI

The inception of the perceptron by Frank Rosenblatt in 1957 marked a seminal moment in the history of artificial intelligence (AI). This early form of neural network was envisioned as a computational model capable of mimicking the decision-making processes observed in the human brain, a concept that remains at the heart of machine learning and AI development today (Banoula, 2021). Rosenblatt's perceptron was groundbreaking, introducing the possibility that machines could not only process information but also learn from data and make predictions based on that learning. This was a radical departure from the rigid, rule-based programming that had dominated computing up until that point, suggesting a path toward machines that could adapt and improve over time.

However, the promise of perceptrons was met with significant challenges. In 1969, Marvin Minsky and Seymour Papert published a critique that exposed fundamental limitations in the perceptron model. Their analysis revealed that perceptrons were incapable of processing XOR (exclusive OR) logic, a simple linear problem, which severely limited their applicability to complex tasks (Fedde, 2016). This critique had a profound impact on the field of AI, leading to what is often referred to as the first "AI winter"—a period of reduced funding and interest in AI research. The work of Minsky and Papert highlighted the necessity for more sophisticated models and approaches, setting the stage for the eventual development of multi-layer neural networks and deep learning technologies that would overcome these early limitations.

Cybernetics, a field pioneered by Norbert Wiener in the 1940s, has been instrumental in shaping the foundational principles of AI. Cybernetics explores the dynamics of control and communication in animals, humans, and machines, introducing the critical concepts of feedback loops and systems theory to the study of intelligent behavior (Nanni, 2023). Wiener's work emphasized the interconnectedness of control and communication processes, positing that effective control systems require feedback to adapt and optimize their behavior over time. These principles have deeply influenced AI research, providing a theoretical framework for understanding how artificial systems can process information, learn from interactions, and adapt to changing environments (Pillar, 2021).

The legacy of cybernetics in AI is profound, offering valuable insights into the nature of intelligence and the mechanisms by which it can be replicated and augmented through technology. By examining the feedback processes and adaptive capabilities inherent in biological and mechanical systems, cybernetics has paved the way for the development of AI algorithms that mimic these natural processes. As AI continues to evolve, the principles of cybernetics remain central to our quest to create intelligent machines that can navigate the complexities of the real world with autonomy and precision.

IMPORTANCE OF AI IN TODAY'S WORLD

Today, AI's importance cannot be overstated. Its applications permeate every aspect of our lives, from enhancing productivity and decision-making to revolutionizing healthcare and addressing environmental challenges. AI's ability to analyze vast datasets, identify patterns, and make predictions has opened new avenues for innovation and problem-solving across various sectors (Fernandes, 2023).

The advancements in AI also bring forth discussions on ethics, privacy, and the future of work, underscoring the need for a balanced approach to AI development and deployment. As AI continues to evolve, it is imperative to consider its societal implications and ensure that its benefits are widely accessible and ethically aligned with human values (Nextech3D.ai, 2023).

Generative AI: The New Frontier

Generative AI represents the latest iteration of AI, pushing the boundaries of creativity and innovation. Unlike traditional AI, which focuses on analyzing and interpreting data, generative AI can create new, original content, ranging from art and music to text and beyond (*What Is Generative AI?*, n.d.). This ability to generate novel outputs from existing data sets opens up unprecedented opportunities for personalization, automation, and creativity across industries.

However, generative AI's capabilities also introduce challenges, such as ensuring accuracy, mitigating bias, and protecting intellectual property. As we explore the potential of generative AI, it is crucial to navigate these challenges with a focus on ethical considerations and responsible use (McKinsey & Company, 2023).

From initial brain-inspired influences to the birth of AI as a scientific field, we've traversed its ups and downs to the emergence of generative AI. The evolution of AI reflects a continuous dialogue between human intellectual curiosity and technological innovation, a testament to our enduring quest to extend the capabilities of our minds through machines.

We will now explore the historical milestones in AI development, tracing the path from early theories to the sophisticated algorithms and systems that define AI today. This historical perspective will not only provide context for AI's current state but also illuminate the potential directions for its future growth.

NAVIGATING THE MILESTONES: THE EVOLUTIONARY JOURNEY OF AI

The evolutionary journey of AI unfolds as a captivating narrative, rich with innovation, ambition, and an unyielding drive to unravel the mysteries of intelligence. This comprehensive timeline offers an interactive exploration of the pivotal milestones in AI development, mapping the field's progression from its conceptual beginnings to the sophisticated systems of 2024.

The Genesis: Early Theories and Computational Models

- **1950**: Alan Turing's introduction of the Turing Test sets the stage, challenging the perceived boundaries between human and machine intelligence (Anyoha, 2017).
- **1956**: The Dartmouth Summer Research Project, a collaborative effort by John McCarthy, Marvin Minsky, Nathaniel Rochester, and Claude Shannon, marks the official birth of AI as a distinct field, laying the foundation for decades of research and development (Karjian, 2023).

The Age of Perceptrons and Early Learning Models

- **1957**: Frank Rosenblatt's invention of the perceptron provides a computational model for pattern recognition, representing an early form of neural networks and a significant stride in the AI journey (Ayyagari, 2020).
- **1967**: The introduction of the "nearest neighbor" algorithm enables computers to start utilizing basic pattern recognition, expanding the scope of AI's capabilities (Karjian, 2023).

The Rise of Machine Learning and Expert Systems

- **1980**: The emergence of expert systems simulates the decision-making abilities of human experts, marking a pivotal advance in AI's practical applications (SITN, 2017).
- **1986**: The popularization of the backpropagation algorithm revolutionizes neural networks, leading to substantial developments in machine learning (Ayyagari, 2020).

The Era of the Internet and Big Data

- **1997**: IBM's Deep Blue defeats world chess champion Garry Kasparov, showcasing AI's prowess in complex, strategic tasks (Karjian, 2023).
- **2006**: Geoffrey Hinton's introduction of "deep learning" signifies a major breakthrough, teaching computers to learn in ways akin to human learning (Ayyagari, 2020).

The Decade of AI Democratization and Ethical AI

- **2011**: IBM's Watson clinches victory in Jeopardy!, demonstrating AI's potential in processing and analyzing extensive datasets (Anyoha, 2017).
- **2014**: Google's DeepMind develops AlphaGo, an AI program that defeats a professional Go player, a feat previously anticipated to be years away (Karjian, 2023).

The Current Landscape: Generative AI and Beyond

- **2020**: OpenAI introduces GPT-3, showcasing advanced capabilities in language understanding and generation (Ayyagari, 2020).
- **2022**: AI models begin demonstrating proficiency in art and music creation, hinting at the burgeoning potential of generative AI (Karjian, 2023).
- **2024**: Presently, AI stands at a reflective and forward-looking juncture. Ethical considerations, transparency, and finding a balance between automation and human labor dominate the discourse. New AI models continue to push the boundaries of what AI can achieve while society grapples with the implications of these advanced technologies.

Throughout this chapter, we've admired the intricacies of the human brain, recognized its influence on AI's early development, and witnessed AI's growth from foundational concepts to its current prominence, including the creative realms of generative AI. We've seen AI's progress as a reflection of our own quest for understanding and innovation, highlighting the symbiotic relationship between human intelligence and AI.

Now, as we transition to *The Foundations of Artificial Intelligence*, we're ready to delve deeper into AI's building blocks, exploring foundational theories, dissecting core components, and unraveling mechanisms that enable AI to learn, reason, and interact. This exploration is not just about enhancing technical knowledge; it's about appreciating the profound connection between human cognition and AI.

In this continuous journey of discovery, each insight leads us forward, reflecting our collective narrative of growth, resilience, and potential. As we turn the page to the next chapter, we carry with us a spirit of inquiry, a commitment to ethical stewardship, and a vision to harness AI's power for the betterment of humanity and our shared future.

2

FOUNDATIONS OF ARTIFICIAL INTELLIGENCE

In the intricate dance of modern business, understanding the steps that lead customers away—a phenomenon known as customer churn—can transform the rhythm of success. The spotlight shines on machine learning, a beacon of hope in the vast sea of data, guiding companies to not just navigate but to thrive in competitive waters by pinpointing the whispers of dissatisfaction before they become waves of departure.

Consider the journey of a telecommunications company caught in the churn's current, watching valuable customers drift away. The deployment of machine learning algorithms became their lighthouse, illuminating the complex patterns hidden within the depths of customer data—usage trends, service feedback, and billing anomalies. This insight was more than a beacon; it was a map to uncharted territories of customer loyalty. By identifying the signs of churn, the company could navigate the troubled waters, reaching out to at-risk customers with the lifelines of personalized incentives and tailored service improvements. The result? A significant reduction in churn, a richer understanding of the customer voyage, and a strategic compass pointing towards long-term engagement.

This narrative is not just a success story; it's a testament to the transformative power of machine learning within the broader realm of AI. Machine learning stands as a cornerstone of AI, a field that stretches beyond the horizon of traditional computing into the realm of adaptive, predictive intelligence. It's where statistical models breathe life into raw data, crafting insights that inform, engage, and inspire action without the confines of explicit programming.

Yet, machine learning represents merely a single chapter in the expansive story of AI. This chapter invites you on an odyssey to explore the confluence of human intuition and machine intellect. It's a tale of merging paths and diverging destinies, where the dreams of yesterday become the realities of today and the possibilities of tomorrow. As we embark on this journey, we delve into the heart of AI, celebrating each discovery as a step closer to understanding the essence of intelligence—both ours and the machines.

WHAT IS MACHINE LEARNING?

In the realm of digital evolution, imagine a scenario where your interactions with technology become increasingly intuitive as if your devices understand you better with each use. This is not a glimpse into a distant future but a present reality underpinned by the transformative power of machine learning. A pivotal branch of artificial intelligence, machine learning equips computers with the remarkable ability to learn and evolve from experience, much like humans absorbing knowledge over time. Through machine learning, applications enhance their functionality, making more accurate predictions and adapting their responses to better meet user needs with each interaction (IBM, 2023).

The Core Pillars of Machine Learning

Machine learning, the bedrock of contemporary AI, is built upon several key concepts that together form the intricate ecosystem enabling machines to acquire, adapt, and refine their intelligence. Let's explore these foundational pillars, each contributing vitally to the symphony of machine learning. Machine learning's foundation is built on several key concepts:

- **Algorithms**: The architects of learning, dictating how machines interpret data.
- **Data**: The cornerstone, acting as the primary source from which machines learn.
- **Features**: The essence of prediction is determining the aspects of data that are most predictive of outcomes.
- **Models**: The culmination of learning, embodying the knowledge gained from data.
- **Training**: The process of refining, where models learn from data to make accurate predictions.

MACHINE LEARNING IN ACTION: A SYMPHONY OF HUMAN AND TECHNOLOGICAL HARMONY

In the panorama of technological advancements, machine learning stands as a monumental pillar, not merely as an element of AI but as a beacon guiding us through the intricacies of human-like learning by machines. This section endeavors to illuminate the essence of machine learning, exploring its diverse landscapes—from supervised to unsupervised and reinforcement learning—and highlighting its profound influence across sectors such as healthcare, finance, retail, travel, and social media. Here, we embark on a journey to understand how machine learning harmonizes technology with human endeavors, transforming the abstract into tangible benefits that touch the core of our daily lives.

Supervised Learning: The Guided Path Through Data's Labyrinth

Picture yourself navigating a labyrinth, where each turn is informed by a guide who knows the maze inside out. Supervised learning mirrors this guided journey, where algorithms traverse the complex landscape of data, illuminated by examples that come paired with both inputs and outputs. This learning style allows models to predict outcomes with increasing accuracy, akin to a student's growth under a mentor's tutelage. The real-world implications are profound:

- **Healthcare**: Supervised learning has revolutionized the way we approach patient care, enabling early interventions and personalized treatment plans through predictive diagnostics (Akhtar, 2023). This technology acts as a diagnostic superpower, preemptively addressing health concerns and potentially saving lives.
- **Finance**: In the financial sector, supervised learning enhances security and trust by powering advanced fraud detection systems. These systems scrutinize transactions to identify anomalies indicative of fraudulent activities, thus safeguarding assets and consumer trust (West & Allen, 2018).
- **Retail**: The retail experience is personalized like never before, with algorithms predicting consumer preferences and tailoring recommendations. It's akin to having a personal shopper who understands your tastes and preferences intimately (Akhtar, 2023).

Unsupervised Learning: Unveiling the Uncharted

Embark on an expedition into the unknown, much like an archeologist discovering hidden relics without a map. Unsupervised learning thrives on its ability to uncover patterns and structures within unlabeled data, revealing insights previously obscured. This autonomous exploration is pivotal in the following ways:

- **Retail**: Customer segmentation is refined to an art form, grouping consumers based on behaviors and preferences, enabling targeted marketing that resonates deeply with each segment's desires (IBM Data and AI Team, 2023).
- **Social Media**: Unsupervised learning parses through the vast digital conversations on social media, performing sentiment analysis that offers brands a nuanced understanding of public opinion (Akhtar, 2023).

Reinforcement Learning: The Game of Strategic Decisions

Imagine engaging in a strategic game where every decision shapes the journey. Reinforcement learning epitomizes this dynamic environment, where algorithms learn from the outcomes of their actions, guided by rewards for beneficial decisions. This learning style excels in the following:

- **Travel**: Optimizing travel experiences by suggesting personalized routes and activities, ensuring an itinerary that aligns with real-time conditions and personal preferences (Akhtar, 2023).

- **Finance**: Navigating the tumultuous seas of stock trading, where algorithms learn to make strategic decisions that maximize returns, much like a seasoned trader interpreting market signals (West & Allen, 2018).

A Canvas of Machine Learning Applications

Machine learning paints a vibrant canvas across various sectors, where each stroke adds depth and color to our digital era's portrait:

- **Healthcare** sees machine learning not just as a tool for diagnostics but as a strategic partner in managing resources and pioneering drug discovery (Akhtar, 2023).
- **Finance** is redefined with AI-driven chatbots that offer round-the-clock assistance, transforming customer service into a seamless, personalized experience (West & Allen, 2018).
- **Retail** benefits from predictive models that ensure inventory efficiency, enhancing consumer satisfaction by ensuring product availability while minimizing waste (Akhtar, 2023).
- **Travel** experiences are personalized to an unprecedented degree, with machine learning crafting recommendations that cater to individual tastes, revolutionizing the planning and enjoyment of travel (Akhtar, 2023).
- **Social Media** platforms leverage machine learning to curate content, ensuring users engage with topics

> that align with their interests, thus enhancing satisfaction and platform loyalty (Akhtar, 2023).

Technology is not merely about emulating human intelligence but about enriching and extending its potential. Through the lens of supervised, unsupervised, and reinforcement learning, we witness the transformative ways in which machine learning revolutionizes industries, amplifies human capabilities, and opens doors to innovation previously unimagined. This exploration serves as a testament to the symbiotic relationship between human ingenuity and technological advancement, highlighting machine learning as a cornerstone of modern artificial intelligence that seamlessly integrates into the tapestry of our lives.

NEURAL NETWORKS AND DEEP LEARNING

Neural networks, at their essence, represent a digital homage to the human brain's architecture, composed of layers of interconnected nodes or "neurons," each meticulously engineered to execute specific computations. This digital fabric processes input data through a hierarchical series of steps, akin to the brain's method of transforming sensory inputs into complex decisions and actions. The design and functionality of neural networks mark a significant departure from traditional computational methodologies, which rely on a set of predetermined rules and instructions for task execution. Instead, neural networks adopt a more fluid, adaptive approach, learning directly from data (IBM Data and AI Team, 2023). This attribute enables them to excel in identifying patterns and deducing insights from the information they're fed, much like assembling a jigsaw puzzle without the guiding image on the box. This capacity for pattern recognition and inference empowers neural networks to tackle problems that defy simple algorithmic solutions, heralding a new era in problem-solving within the digital domain.

The advent of neural networks has imbued machines with the remarkable ability to learn from experiences, adapt to new scenarios, and make informed decisions with minimal oversight. This breakthrough not only augments the capabilities of AI systems but also expands their applicability across various domains, pushing the boundaries of what machines can achieve and how they can augment human endeavors (IBM Data and AI Team, 2023).

Deep Learning: The Evolutionary Leap in AI

Deep learning signifies an evolutionary leap in the journey of AI, refining the concept of neural networks into a more profound paradigm. Characterized by the integration of multiple layers, hence the term "deep," deep learning facilitates the processing and interpretation of data with an unprecedented level of complexity and abstraction. It has propelled significant breakthroughs across various fields, from enhancing natural language processing to pioneering autonomous navigation, all made possible by the system's ability to learn from extensive datasets in a manner reminiscent of human cognition (IBM Data and AI Team, 2023).

The inception of deep learning has ignited a revolution across diverse domains, making tasks like precise image recognition and sophisticated speech interpretation not only feasible but remarkably accurate. The essence of deep learning lies in its unparalleled ability to identify complex patterns within large volumes of data, establishing it as the cornerstone of contemporary AI advancements.

The transformative impact of deep learning on AI is profound, opening avenues for myriad new possibilities and applications. Its advanced pattern recognition capabilities, coupled with the ability to learn from extensive datasets, have accelerated AI's progress, driving innovations that once bordered on the realm of science fiction (IBM Data and AI Team, 2023).

Deciphering Neural Networks: Understanding the Mechanics

At the foundation of neural networks lies a sophisticated mechanism that echoes the cognitive functions of the human brain, converting raw data into actionable insights. This intricate process begins with introducing data into a layered architecture of interconnected nodes, often referred to as artificial neurons. Each neuron undertakes the critical task of applying specific weights and biases to the input data, funneling it through an activation function that dictates the signal's progression through the network. This iterative process, akin to refining a skill through practice, is pivotal for the model's ability to accurately predict or classify data (AWS, n.d.).

From Machine Learning to Deep Learning: Unveiling the Distinction

While machine learning and deep learning are often mentioned in tandem, they represent distinct concepts within the broader AI landscape. Machine learning encompasses a wide array of techniques for enabling computers to learn from and make predictions based on data, including but not limited to neural networks. Deep learning, by contrast, refers specifically to the use of deep neural networks for this purpose (IBM, 2023).

One key distinction between the two is their reliance on data volume for improving accuracy. Deep learning models need significantly more data to fine-tune their accuracy compared to traditional machine learning models due to deep learning models' ability to learn and extract features directly from the data, necessitating a comprehensive dataset to cover the vast complexity these models can handle (IBM Data and AI Team, 2023).

This exploration into neural networks and deep learning not only sheds light on the technical underpinnings of these AI technologies but also underscores their significance in propelling the field forward. By understanding how these systems work and their impact on the development of AI, we gain insights into the future possibilities that neural networks and deep learning hold, driving a wave of innovations that could redefine our interaction with technology and further blur the lines between biological intelligence and artificial prowess.

NATURAL LANGUAGE PROCESSING

In the vanguard of AI, Natural Language Processing (NLP) emerges as a transformative force, redefining the interface between humanity and the digital realm. At its core, NLP encapsulates the discipline that equips machines with the ability to comprehend, interpret, and articulate human language in a manner that is both significant and utilitarian. This synergy between linguistic intricacies and computational prowess enables the processing and analysis of vast troves of natural language data, effectively bridging the communicative divide that has long separated human expressiveness from the binary world of machines.

Occupying the intersection of computer science, artificial intelligence, and linguistics, NLP crafts sophisticated systems that parse text and speech, mirroring human levels of understanding. It delves into the structural and semantic intricacies of language, enabling machines to dissect and interpret complex linguistic constructs. By employing a range of analytical techniques — from parsing, which unravels the grammatical structure of sentences, to stemming, which reduces words to their root form — NLP breaks down language into its fundamental components. This dissection process is crucial for machines to grasp the syntax and semantics of the text, setting the stage for more elaborate tasks of language processing and understanding (TechTarget Contributor, 2024).

Expanding the Horizons of Human-Machine Communication

Beyond mere text analysis, the importance of NLP lies in its capacity to significantly enhance the interaction between humans and machines, making it more intuitive and engaging. By equipping machines with the ability to understand and articulate human language, NLP opens up a realm of possibilities for performing tasks that once required human intellect. From translating languages in real-time and enabling seamless cross-cultural communication to facilitating advanced customer service interactions through chatbots, NLP significantly widens the scope and accessibility of digital services and information.

From Theory to Practice: NLP at Work

The practical application of NLP techniques transforms unstructured text into structured, analyzable data. This transformation is pivotal in a myriad of applications, such as text classification, which organizes documents into predefined categories, facilitating efficient content management and retrieval. Similarly, text extraction pulls specific pieces of information from larger texts, enabling targeted analysis. Machine translation, a hallmark application of NLP, dissolves linguistic barriers, while natural language generation crafts coherent, human-like text from data sets, powering news generation, report writing, and more. Each of these applications exemplifies NLP's transformative potential in making language-based data more accessible, actionable, and engaging.

NLP's capacity to automate, refine, and innovate the processing of natural language data is vividly shown in multiple key scenarios, showcasing its versatility and utility.

- **Spam Detection:** Email services efficiently sift through and eliminate spam Using text classification, markedly enhancing both user experience and digital security.
- **Machine Translation:** Tools like Google Translate leverage NLP for instant language translation, fostering unhindered global communication and accessibility to information.
- **Virtual Agents and Chatbots:** Powered by NLP, chatbots have revolutionized customer service, offering precise, understandable responses to inquiries 24/7, ensuring consistent user support.
- **Social Media Sentiment Analysis:** NLP enables brands to analyze sentiment on social platforms, extracting consumer insights from vast quantities of user-generated content to inform marketing and product strategies.
- **Text Summarization:** By automatically condensing extensive documents into concise summaries, NLP aids in efficient information consumption, particularly in documentation-heavy fields such as law and academia.

These examples underscore the profound influence of NLP across various sectors, showcasing its role in streamlining communication, enhancing information accessibility, and facilitating deeper, more meaningful human-machine interactions.

As NLP continues to evolve, driven by the latest advancements in machine learning and deep learning, its applications are poised to become even more integrated into our daily lives, redefining the landscape of digital communication. This progression of NLP is not merely about augmenting the capabilities of machines but is aimed at forging a future where technology can fully comprehend, respond to, and participate in human linguistic exchanges. Envisioning a world where machines understand the subtleties of human language, NLP stands at the forefront of creating a more connected, accessible, and enriched communicative experience, heralding a new era of interaction where the boundaries between human intellect and artificial intelligence become increasingly blurred.

HARNESSING THE ESSENCE OF AI: A PRELUDE TO EVERYDAY APPLICATIONS

To encapsulate the wealth of knowledge explored in this chapter and enhance your understanding, we present an interactive summary. These snapshot boxes provide a distilled overview of the pivotal areas within artificial intelligence that are reshaping our world.

Types of Machine Learning: A Spectrum of Learning Strategies

- **Supervised Learning:** Like a student learning under the guidance of a teacher, this method relies on labeled datasets to teach models how to predict outcomes based on input-output pairs. It's pivotal in areas like healthcare for disease prediction and retail for personalized shopping experiences.

- **Unsupervised Learning:** This method explores data without explicit instructions, identifying hidden patterns and relationships. It excels in retail customer segmentation and discovering insights within vast datasets, like those encountered in social media analytics.
- **Reinforcement Learning:** Mimicking a trial-and-error learning process, this strategy rewards or penalizes algorithms based on their actions' outcomes, optimizing decision-making in dynamic environments such as gaming strategies and financial trading.

Neural Networks: Simulating the Human Brain's Intricacy

Neural networks, inspired by the human brain's structure, consist of layers of nodes that process data in a hierarchical manner. These networks excel at recognizing patterns and making inferences, allowing computers to tackle complex tasks without explicit programming. They form the backbone of many AI applications, from voice recognition systems to predictive analytics.

Deep Learning: Advancing Beyond Traditional Boundaries

Deep learning, a subset of machine learning, utilizes multi-layered neural networks to analyze data with unprecedented depth and complexity. It powers groundbreaking advancements in fields such as computer vision for image recognition and natural language processing for understanding human language. Deep learning models thrive on large datasets, extracting features and learning patterns directly from the data.

Natural Language Processing (NLP): Bridging Human Communication with AI

NLP enables machines to understand, interpret, and generate human language, facilitating a range of applications that require nuanced linguistic handling. Key methods include:

- **Parsing and Word Segmentation:** Breaking down sentences into their grammatical components and separating text into individual words for deeper analysis.
- **Sentence Breaking and Morphological Segmentation:** Dividing text into sentences and analyzing word structures to understand their roots and variations.
- **Stemming:** Reducing words to their base or root form, simplifying linguistic analysis.

This exploration into AI's core constructs not only illuminates the mechanisms driving today's innovations but also underscores the significance of grasping these concepts for anyone looking to navigate the AI-infused future. As we pivot from the foundational aspects of AI to its applications in the ensuing chapter, I aim to show how deeply AI is interwoven into the fabric of our daily existence, from smart homes that adapt to our preferences to AI-driven health monitors that guard our well-being.

Chapter 3 promises an insightful journey into the practical applications of AI, revealing how the technologies discussed here enhance our homes, streamline our tasks, and enrich our leisure, thereby transforming abstract concepts into tangible benefits. This transition underscores the vitality of understanding AI's foundational elements as a means to fully appreciate and leverage the technology in enhancing our daily lives.

By demystifying the core principles of AI, we lay the groundwork for a deeper exploration of its techniques and applications, emphasizing the transformative potential of AI in reshaping our interactions with technology. As we move forward, the exploration of AI's role in home and everyday life not only highlights the practical benefits of these technologies but also invites us to consider the future possibilities they herald. In this journey through AI's application, we are reminded of the power of technology to not only solve complex problems but also to make our daily experiences more connected, efficient, and personalized.

3

UTILIZING AI AT HOME AND IN EVERYDAY LIFE

In December 2022, the Pew Research Center conducted a survey of 11,004 U.S. adults, revealing a fascinating insight into our daily interactions with AI. The survey found that 27% of Americans say they interact with AI at least several times a day, while another 28% believe they engage with it about once a day or several times a week. Interestingly, a significant 44% of respondents think they do not regularly interact with AI (Kennedy et al., 2023). This statistic paints a compelling picture of the paradox that exists between the actual prevalence of AI in our daily lives and our awareness of these interactions.

The pervasive nature of AI technology, seemingly invisible yet integral to our daily routines, underscores a critical gap in public perception. While many of us envision AI as the stuff of science fiction—autonomous robots or sophisticated supercomputers—the reality is that AI is much more ingrained in the mundane aspects of our everyday existence. From the moment we ask our digital assistants to set an alarm to the way our social media feeds are curated, AI is quietly shaping our daily experiences, often in ways we scarcely notice.

This chapter aims to bridge this awareness gap by shedding light on the myriad ways AI integrates into our homes and personal routines. Far from the futuristic scenarios we might imagine, AI's current role is both practical and deeply intertwined with our everyday activities. It's in the voice-activated devices that play our favorite songs on command, the smart thermostats that learn our preferences to optimize home comfort and energy use, and the personalized recommendations that guide our entertainment choices.

The goal here is not just to catalog these interactions but to illuminate the sophisticated algorithms and machine learning models that power them. By doing so, we hope to foster a deeper understanding of how AI technologies enhance convenience, personalize experiences, and support us in areas as diverse as health, entertainment, and education. This exploration is vital for two reasons: firstly, to appreciate the invisible yet impactful role AI plays in making our daily lives more efficient and enjoyable, and secondly, to encourage a more informed and nuanced conversation about AI's potential and its future direction.

As we delve into the specifics of AI's applications in the following sections, keep in mind that the technology's true marvel lies not in its ability to replicate human intelligence but in its capacity to augment our daily lives in subtle yet profound ways. The journey through the various forms AI takes in our homes and personal routines is not just an exploration of technology; it's a reflection of how innovation continuously reshapes our interaction with the world around us. In recognizing and understanding these interactions, we can better navigate the benefits and challenges that AI presents, ensuring that we harness its potential to improve not just our personal lives but also the broader fabric of society.

INTEGRATION OF AI IN SMART HOMES

The integration of AI in smart homes marks a revolutionary stride towards creating living spaces that are not only efficient and secure but also deeply personalized. This transformation is largely driven by the seamless incorporation of AI technologies across various home devices, enhancing the quality of daily life by making homes smarter, more responsive, and intuitively aligned with individual preferences and needs.

From voice-activated assistants that manage household tasks to smart thermostats that adapt to our routines, AI is the driving force behind the creation of homes that understand us better than ever before. The integration of AI into smart homes not only enhances efficiency but also brings about a level of personalization that was previously unimaginable. Devices can learn from our behaviors, adapt to our preferences, and even anticipate our needs, making our homes not just places of residence but partners in our daily lives.

By Type

The variety of AI-enabled devices available today is vast, each serving different aspects of home life:

- **Smart Speakers with AI Integration**: Devices like Amazon Echo and Google Home have become central to the AI-powered home, offering voice-activated assistance for everything from playing music to providing weather updates.
- **AI-Enabled Smart Thermostats**: Thermostats like Nest learn your temperature preferences and adjust automatically, optimizing home comfort and energy use.
- **AI-Powered Smart Lighting Systems**: Lighting systems that adjust based on time of day, presence in the room, or even mood, all controllable via voice or smartphone apps.
- **AI-Integrated Security Cameras and Systems**: Enhanced security features like facial recognition and unusual activity alerts provide peace of mind

with a level of convenience and personalization traditional systems cannot match.
- **AI-Enhanced Smart Appliances**: Refrigerators that can inventory their contents and suggest recipes or washing machines that optimize water and energy use based on load size are examples of how AI is transforming household chores.

By Application

The applications of AI in smart home technology are diverse, covering a broad spectrum of household needs:

- **Voice Assistance and Command Recognition**: AI assistants can control smart devices, set reminders, and even make purchases online, acting as the central hub of the smart home.
- **Energy Management and Optimization**: Smart thermostats and lighting systems use AI to reduce energy consumption, learning from your habits to create the most efficient schedules.
- **Home Security and Surveillance**: AI-driven cameras and alarm systems offer real-time monitoring with intelligent threat detection and alerts.
- **Ambient Intelligence and Context Awareness**: Devices that adjust settings based on the current environment or user's activity, providing an intuitive living experience.
- **Predictive Maintenance and Fault Detection**: Smart appliances that alert you to potential issues

before they become major problems, saving time and money on repairs.

By Connectivity

The effectiveness of AI in smart homes is significantly enhanced by connectivity options. Wi-Fi-enabled devices remain popular, but Bluetooth-connected gadgets, Zigbee/Z-Wave supported devices, cellular connectivity, and even Ethernet-connected appliances are integral to creating a cohesive, fully integrated smart home ecosystem. This connectivity ensures that AI technologies can communicate seamlessly with each other, creating a network of devices that work in concert to cater to the homeowner's needs.

By End-User

While residential applications are the most commonly associated with smart home technologies, the use of AI extends to commercial settings like hotels and offices and even industrial applications in smart buildings. AI-integrated healthcare facilities and assisted living homes are leveraging these technologies to provide better care and enhanced living conditions for residents.

Key Market Players

The smart home technology market is buoyed by major companies such as Google (Nest), Amazon (Ring), Apple (HomeKit), and Samsung (SmartThings), whose innovations have been pivotal in bringing AI into the mainstream of home living. Other significant contributors include Philips

(Hue) for smart lighting, LG (ThinQ) for smart appliances, and iRobot (Roomba) for cleaning, each playing a critical role in advancing smart home technologies. These companies, among others, have not only pushed the boundaries of what's possible with AI in our homes but have also made these technologies accessible to a wider audience.

In conclusion, AI's role in smart home technologies is transformative, offering a glimpse into a future where our homes are not just places of shelter but intelligent environments that enhance our daily lives in myriad ways. As these technologies evolve and become even more integrated into our homes, the potential for even greater efficiency, personalization, and convenience is boundless. The journey into the AI-enhanced home is just beginning, promising a future where our living spaces are in perfect harmony with our needs and preferences.

SMART HOME TECHNOLOGIES

Embarking on the journey of transforming your living space into a smart home is akin to stepping into a future where your home not only understands your needs but anticipates them, thanks to the marvels of AI. The integration of AI into smart homes is not just an upgrade; it's a revolution that redefines the essence of home living, making efficiency and personalization paramount.

A Glimpse into AI-Enabled Devices

Imagine walking into your home, and with just a simple voice command, the lights dim to your preferred setting, your favorite music begins to play, and the thermostat adjusts to the perfect temperature. This is not the future; it's the present, powered by **AI-enabled smart speakers** like Amazon Alexa and Google Assistant. These devices once considered novelties, have now become the heart of the smart home ecosystem, acting as the central command center from which a web of interconnected devices operates (Future Data Stats, 2023).

AI-enabled smart thermostats, such as Nest or Ecobee, go beyond mere temperature control. It learns your schedule and preferences, ensuring your home is always at the ideal temperature when you're there and conserving energy when you're not (Guest Writer, 2023). Then, there's the **AI-powered smart lighting system** by Philips Hue, which not only allows you to control lighting with your voice but also learns from your habits to create the perfect ambiance for every moment.

Home security, a major concern for homeowners, has been transformed by the integration of AI into **security cameras and systems.** These aren't just recording devices; they're intelligent sentinels capable of distinguishing between a falling leaf and a potential intruder, ensuring peace of mind.

And let's not forget the **AI-enhanced smart appliances**, from refrigerators that suggest recipes based on their contents to washing machines that optimize water and detergent use based on the laundry load. These devices are not just about convenience; they're about personalizing your home life to suit your unique lifestyle (Future Data Stats, 2023).

Transforming the Home Environment through AI Applications

The magic of AI in smart homes extends beyond the devices themselves to the experiences they enable. **Voice assistance** has turned from a futuristic fantasy into a daily convenience, allowing us to interact with our homes in the most natural way possible - through conversation (Future Data Stats, 2023).

Energy management through AI doesn't just cut costs; it contributes to a more sustainable world, optimizing energy use and reducing waste. Similarly, **home security** systems now offer more than alarms; they provide insights, sending alerts only when there's a genuine concern, thus blending security with serenity.

The concept of **ambient intelligence** brings a layer of context-awareness to our homes, making them not just spaces we live in but spaces that live with us, adapting to our moods, activities, and preferences[9].

The Significance of Connectivity

The seamless integration of these AI devices into a cohesive ecosystem is made possible through a variety of connectivity options, from Wi-Fi and Bluetooth to Zigbee/Z-Wave and Ethernet. This network of connectivity options ensures that no matter the device, it can become a part of the larger smart home system, offering a unified and harmonious living experience.

Beyond the Home: AI's Expanding Reach

The impact of AI in smart technologies is not confined to residential spaces. From **commercial settings** like hotels and offices to **industrial environments**, AI is enhancing experiences, productivity, and safety across a broad spectrum of applications. In commercial spaces, it's about creating memorable experiences for guests; in industrial settings, it's about ensuring operations run smoothly and safely.

The Visionaries Behind AI Smart Homes

The landscape of AI in smart homes is shaped by key market players such as **Google (Nest)**, **Amazon (Ring)**, and **Apple (HomeKit)**. These innovators are not just creating products; they're crafting experiences and pushing the boundaries of what a smart home can be (Guest Writer, 2023). Their relentless pursuit of innovation ensures that the smart home technology market is always evolving, offering new ways to enhance our living spaces.

As we delve deeper into the world of smart home technologies, it's clear that AI is not just a tool; it's a companion that makes our lives more comfortable, secure, and efficient. Integrating AI into our homes is a personal journey that reflects our desire for an intelligent living space that enhances our quality of life. This chapter is not just about understanding the technologies that make this possible; it's about envisioning how they can transform our everyday experiences, making every moment at home an instance of personalized comfort and convenience.

Understanding AI Assistants

AI assistants, also known as virtual assistants, are software agents that can perform tasks or services for an individual based on commands or questions. Powered by artificial intelligence, these assistants process natural language to interact with users in a way that mimics human conversation, making technology more accessible and intuitive than ever before (Yasar, n.d.). They leverage advanced AI technologies, including machine learning, natural language processing, and voice recognition, to understand and predict user needs (*What Is an AI Assistant?*, 2023).

The core functionality of AI assistants revolves around their ability to process and interpret human speech, turning spoken commands into actions. Whether it's setting a reminder, playing a song, or controlling smart home devices, AI assistants serve as the intermediary between users and their digital ecosystems, simplifying interactions and enhancing efficiency.

Benefits and Types of AI Assistants

The benefits of incorporating AI assistants into daily life are manifold. They offer **convenience** by performing tasks through simple voice commands, eliminating the need to physically interact with multiple devices or navigate complex menus. **Efficiency** is another significant advantage, as AI assistants can streamline routine tasks, manage schedules, and even automate home management, freeing up valuable time for users. Additionally, they provide **personalized**

experiences by learning from user interactions, tailoring responses, and recommendations to individual preferences.

There are three distinct types of AI assistants, each designed for different purposes:

- **Chatbots** are designed primarily for text-based interaction, offering customer service or information retrieval functions on websites and messaging platforms. They're the simplest form of AI assistants, programmed to respond to specific inquiries with pre-defined answers.
- **Conversational Agents** represent a more advanced interaction level, capable of engaging in dialogues that require understanding context and user intent. These agents are often found in customer support scenarios, providing more personalized and adaptive responses.
- **Virtual Assistants** like Siri, Google Assistant, and Alexa are the most sophisticated, integrating voice recognition and advanced AI to offer comprehensive assistance across a wide range of tasks and services.

Popular AI Assistants and Their Capabilities

Siri: Apple's pioneering virtual assistant, Siri, introduced many to the concept of conversing with their devices. Siri excels in handling a variety of tasks, from sending messages and setting reminders to providing weather updates and navigation assistance. Its integration across Apple's ecosystem allows for a seamless experience across devices (*What Is an AI Assistant?*, 2023).

Google Assistant: Known for its powerful search capabilities, Google Assistant offers users a wide range of functionalities, including controlling smart home devices, accessing information from the web, and managing personal schedules. Its ability to understand natural language and context makes it one of the most intuitive assistants available (McCarthy, n.d.).

Amazon Alexa: Alexa has become synonymous with smart home control, offering compatibility with a vast array of smart devices. Beyond controlling lights or thermostats, Alexa can play music, make shopping lists, and even order products directly from Amazon, making it a cornerstone of convenience for many households (McCarthy, n.d.).

Bixby: Samsung's Bixby focuses on device interaction, offering deep integration with Samsung's smartphones, appliances, and smart TVs. Bixby aims to make device management more intuitive, allowing users to perform complex tasks through simple voice commands (*What Is an AI Assistant?*, 2023).

Incorporating an AI assistant into one's daily routine can dramatically enhance productivity and convenience. By understanding the unique features and strengths of each assistant, users can choose the one that best fits their lifestyle and needs, further personalizing their interaction with technology. As AI technology continues to evolve, the capabilities of these assistants will only grow, further integrating into our daily lives and making the smart home experience more accessible and enjoyable for everyone.

TRANSFORMING ENTERTAINMENT WITH AI

AI is changing the game in the entertainment and media sectors, revolutionizing our experiences with music, movies, gaming, and digital content. By offering personalized experiences and forging new avenues for content creation, AI is not just a technological advancement; it's a paradigm shift in how content is tailored to individual tastes and created with machine efficiency.

Streaming giants like Netflix and Spotify leverage AI to analyze viewing and listening habits, marrying this data with extensive content libraries to craft recommendations that resonate on a personal level. This not only transforms the user experience into a journey of discovery but also challenges the notion of passive consumption (Takyar, 2023). Beyond curation, AI's role in content creation marks a significant leap forward. Innovations in AI-driven music composition and scriptwriting, exemplified by tools like AIVA and Scriptbook, showcase AI's capacity to not only mimic but also amplify human creativity, offering creators new tools to inspire and streamline their artistic processes (Srivastava, 2023b).

The future of AI in entertainment hints at even greater personalization and collaboration. Advancements in machine learning and natural language processing promise to refine recommendation algorithms further, making them more intuitive and context-aware. The emerging trend of human-AI collaboration in content creation suggests a future where AI acts not merely as a tool but as a creative partner, expanding the horizon of possibilities for artists and content creators (Takyar, 2023).

Real-world applications, such as AIVA's ability to compose emotive soundtracks by learning from classical music compositions or Scriptbook's script analysis for predicting a screenplay's success, underline AI's transformative impact on the industry. These examples not only demonstrate AI's ability to grasp and replicate complex creative processes but also highlight its potential to drive innovation and enhance consumer experiences.

As AI continues to evolve, its integration into entertainment and media is set to deepen, offering exciting opportunities for innovation. This synergy between AI and creativity is not just about pushing technological boundaries; it's about reimagining the landscape of content creation and consumption, promising a future where entertainment is more personalized, immersive, and engaging than ever before.

ROLE OF AI IN PERSONAL HEALTH

Through the sophisticated use of data analytics and machine learning algorithms, AI is offering insights specifically tailored to individual health objectives, conditions, and progress. This personalized approach is revolutionizing how we engage with fitness routines, health monitoring, and even nutritional guidance.

In the realm of health and fitness, AI's role is particularly transformative. Fitness applications and wearable technology equipped with AI diligently track a plethora of user activities—from daily steps and heart rate to sleep patterns and exercise regimens. This data, meticulously analyzed over time, enables AI to uncover trends, offer health recommendations, and even anticipate potential health issues, providing a proactive stance toward wellness. Such dynamic personalization not only adapts to the user's immediate feedback and evolving goals but also maximizes the effectiveness of fitness and nutrition strategies, ensuring they grow with the individual.

Noteworthy examples of AI's integration into fitness apps underscore its potential to reshape personal wellness practices. MyFitnessPal utilizes AI to decipher users' dietary and exercise patterns, offering bespoke nutritional and workout advice aimed at achieving specific health milestones. Similarly, Fitbit leverages AI to give insights based on physical activity, sleep, and heart rate data, guiding users towards improved sleep, increased activity, or stress management with personalized recommendations. Strava enhances the social fitness experience with AI, providing tailored training plans and performance analytics to motivate users through communal engagement and competitive benchmarks. Headspace brings AI into mental wellness, customizing meditation, and mindfulness sessions based on user mood and preferences, thereby making mental health practices more accessible and impactful.

These instances vividly illustrate AI's broad applicability across physical activity, nutrition, and mental health, demonstrating its capacity to empower individuals with personalized recommendations, predictive analysis, and real-time feedback. As AI technology evolves, it promises to introduce even more groundbreaking health and fitness solutions, further refining personal wellness experiences and boosting the effectiveness of health monitoring and management. The future of personal health and fitness, deeply intertwined with AI, beckons a new era of precision and support, enabling individuals to achieve their wellness objectives with unparalleled accuracy.

THE IMPACT OF AI ON PROFESSIONAL DEVELOPMENT

AI is reshaping professional development by delivering personalized learning, optimizing workflows, and generating insights for intelligent decision-making. AI's ability to analyze large data sets enables professionals to access tailored learning resources, streamline processes, and improve strategic capabilities, ushering in a new era of career growth and skill development.

- **Personalized Learning Plans with AI**: AI excels in crafting personalized learning pathways by assessing an individual's skills, career goals, and industry trends. It recommends relevant courses and adapts to the learner's progress, ensuring a tailored approach to professional growth. This dynamic adaptation not only keeps professionals abreast of evolving industry trends but also aligns learning with personal aspirations, making skill development both targeted and efficient.
- **Enhancing Learning Materials**: AI-powered platforms transform complex information into manageable, bite-sized pieces, aligning with the learner's pace and style. Utilizing natural language processing and machine learning, these platforms curate engaging content, making the learning process not just more accessible but also more enjoyable.

- **Advancing to Higher Concepts**: AI's adaptive learning systems introduce more complex material as learners advance, ensuring ongoing challenge and growth. This ensures that professionals remain at the forefront of their field, equipped with cutting-edge knowledge and skills.
- **AI-Driven Assessments**: Through nuanced assessments, AI provides a deeper understanding of a learner's mastery, pinpointing strengths and areas for improvement. Immediate feedback enables swift adjustments in learning strategies, fostering a more effective educational journey.
- **Discovering Learning Opportunities**: AI extends its benefits beyond digital learning, guiding professionals to conferences, workshops, and networking events that match their career trajectories and interests. By analyzing learning patterns and industry movements, AI spots opportunities for further growth and development.

Integrating AI into Professional Workflows

Incorporating AI into daily work routines significantly boosts productivity and efficiency. From automating mundane tasks to enhancing decision-making, AI tools redefine workplace innovation.

- **Understanding AI Tools**: A preliminary step involves acquainting oneself with the diverse AI technologies available. Knowledge of machine learning algorithms, natural language processing, and AI analytics platforms is essential for leveraging AI's full potential.

- **Identifying AI Opportunities**: Evaluating daily responsibilities to pinpoint where AI can introduce efficiencies is crucial. Opportunities might include automating administrative tasks, enhancing communication, or improving customer interactions through AI-driven solutions.
- **Selecting Suitable AI Tools**: Choosing the right AI tools is pivotal. Factors to consider include user-friendliness, compatibility with existing systems, and specific features that meet professional needs.
- **Starting Small**: Gradual implementation of AI tools allows for a comfortable adjustment period, building confidence in AI's benefits and understanding its impact on workflow.
- **Soliciting Feedback**: Collaborating with peers and soliciting their input on AI integration can offer new perspectives and refine the use of AI in professional settings.

The shift towards AI-driven professional development is not just about staying current in one's field; it's about reimagining the path to professional excellence. As the workplace continues to evolve, AI emerges as a key ally in the pursuit of continuous improvement, efficiency, and innovation, heralding a future where professional growth is both personalized and propelled by intelligent technology.

INTEGRATING AI INTO YOUR DAILY ROUTINE

Embracing AI in our daily lives can seem daunting at first, yet the journey to making AI a personal assistant, health coach, and professional advisor is simpler and more intuitive than you might think. Here's how you can start integrating AI into your daily routine today:

- **Leverage AI Assistants for Daily Tasks**: Begin by using AI assistants like Siri, Google Assistant, or Alexa to set reminders and alarms and create to-do lists. These small steps can introduce you to the convenience of voice-activated commands and the efficiency of having a virtual assistant.
- **Health Tracking and Personalized Fitness**: Explore fitness apps that utilize AI to tailor workout and nutrition plans specifically for you. Apps like Fitbit or MyFitnessPal analyze your activity levels and dietary habits to provide personalized recommendations, helping you achieve your health goals more effectively.
- **Professional Development with AI**: Utilize AI-powered platforms for learning and professional growth. Platforms that offer personalized learning paths based on your career goals and skills can significantly enhance your professional development. Set aside time each week to engage with these platforms, focusing on areas that AI identifies as opportunities for growth.
- **Explore Smart Home Devices**: Experiment with AI-enabled smart home devices, starting with smart speakers or smart lighting systems. These devices

can introduce you to the world of home automation, where convenience, efficiency, and personalization enhance your living space.
- **Feedback and Adaptation**: As you integrate AI into your routine, pay attention to the feedback these systems provide. Many AI tools learn from your interactions, so the more you use them, the better they become at serving your needs.

By taking these actionable steps, you are not simply utilizing technology; you are actually welcoming AI to become a partner in optimizing various aspects of your daily life, health, and professional journey. In the preceding chapter, we have delved into the numerous ways in which AI seamlessly integrates into our daily routines, spanning from the comfort of our homes to our personal health regimens and even our efforts toward professional development. The convenience and personalization that AI brings to our everyday activities highlight its transformative capabilities, ultimately enhancing our efficiency, making our health goals more attainable, and enabling targeted and effective professional growth.

AI's role extends beyond automating tasks; it's about enhancing our human experiences, providing insights that lead to better decisions, and opening up new avenues for personal and professional growth. The exploration of AI-enabled devices, health apps, and learning platforms illustrates the profound impact AI has on enhancing our daily lives, making the technology not just an external tool but a part of our personal and professional narratives.

As we close this chapter on the personal and home applications of AI, we stand at the threshold of a broader exploration of AI's transformative impact across different industries. The following chapter will expand our horizons, exploring how AI is revolutionizing sectors such as health-care, finance, education, and more, further illustrating AI's integral role in shaping our society and the future.

By understanding the personal applications of AI, we've laid the groundwork for appreciating its broader implications. The journey ahead promises to unveil the full spectrum of AI's potential, inviting us to envision a future where AI's contributions transcend individual experiences, driving innovation and progress on a societal scale. As we venture into this exploration, let's carry forward the insights gained from personal applications of AI, ready to appreciate the vast possibilities that AI holds for transforming industries and society at large.

4

AI IN ACTION: REAL-WORLD APPLICATIONS AND CASE STUDIES

> *There's no one thing that defines AI. It's more like a tapestry of modern intelligent technologies knit together in a strategic fashion that can then uplift*

and create a knowledge base that is automated — where you can extrapolate findings from there.

— JOHN FREMONT

This observation encapsulates the essence of AI not as a singular entity but as a constellation of sophisticated technologies that, when woven together, forge a system capable of transforming data into insights, automating complex processes, and enhancing decision-making across numerous sectors. AI's multifaceted nature allows it to seep into the very fabric of various industries, revolutionizing operations, redefining user experiences, and unveiling possibilities previously tethered to the realm of imagination.

AI's integration into real-world applications showcases its remarkable versatility and adaptability. From healthcare, where AI algorithms help diagnose diseases with precision rivaling seasoned professionals, to the financial sector, where it predicts market trends and personalizes customer services, AI's capabilities are vast and varied. In education, AI personalizes learning experiences, adapting in real-time to meet the individual needs of students, while in agriculture, it optimizes crop yields and conserves resources through precise monitoring and predictive analytics.

The chapter ahead delves into these applications and more, illustrating how AI's strategic implementation can uplift industries, streamline operations, and forge a path toward a future where intelligence is not just learned but also shared, enhanced, and leveraged for the greater good. By examining AI's role across different scenarios, we gain insight into its potential to not just automate tasks but to innovate solutions that address complex challenges, making AI a pivotal force in shaping the future.

AI IN HEALTHCARE: A REVOLUTION IN PATIENT CARE AND MEDICAL RESEARCH

The use of AI in healthcare is revolutionizing the delivery and management of medical care. From its nascent applications in digitizing medical records to the current sophisticated algorithms aiding diagnostics, treatment planning, and research, AI's trajectory in healthcare has been both transformative and life-saving. The essence of AI's role in healthcare is its ability to parse through vast datasets—far beyond human capability—identifying patterns, anomalies, and solutions that can significantly improve patient outcomes and operational efficiencies. The introduction of AI into healthcare has not only enhanced the precision and speed of medical services but has also opened new avenues for personalized medicine and preventive care.

One of the most significant impacts of AI in healthcare is in diagnostics, where it aids in the early detection and accurate diagnosis of diseases. AI algorithms, trained on thousands of patient images, can now identify conditions such as cancers, neurological disorders, and cardiovascular diseases with a precision that matches or surpasses that of human experts (Marr, 2018; Georgiou, 2020).

For instance, AI systems used in radiology not only enhance image quality but also help radiologists interpret scans more efficiently, reducing diagnostic errors and improving patient outcomes. In treatment planning, AI's data-driven insights assist healthcare professionals in devising personalized treatment regimens. By analyzing the genetic makeup of tumors, AI algorithms can predict which chemotherapy drugs are likely to be most effective for individual cancer patients, thus optimizing treatment plans and improving survival rates. Moreover, AI supports multidisciplinary collaboration in cancer care, enabling teams to develop comprehensive, personalized treatment strategies based on a wealth of clinical data (Philips, 2022).

AI's contribution to medical research is invaluable, significantly speeding up the drug discovery process and the development of novel therapies. Through the analysis of complex biological datasets, AI helps identify potential drug targets and predicts the efficacy of drug compounds, streamlining the research phase and reducing the time and cost associated with bringing new medications to market (Marr, 2018).

AI applications extend beyond diagnostics and treatment to include operational improvements within healthcare facilities. AI-driven systems forecast patient flow, enabling hospitals to allocate resources more effectively and reduce wait times. Predictive maintenance algorithms minimize equipment downtime, ensuring that vital diagnostic tools are available when needed. In inpatient care, AI monitors vital signs to detect early signs of deterioration, facilitating timely interventions and improving patient safety (Philips, 2022).

Furthermore, AI has enabled remote monitoring and minimally invasive procedures, enhancing patient care and accessibility. Remote monitoring systems equipped with AI technology can track patients' vital signs and detect any abnormalities, allowing healthcare providers to intervene promptly. AI-assisted robotic surgeries enable surgeons to perform complex procedures with greater precision and accuracy, minimizing invasiveness and reducing recovery times.

This merger has revolutionized various aspects of the industry, from diagnostics and treatment planning to operational improvements and patient care. Its ability to enhance precision, speed, and personalized medicine holds great promise for the future of healthcare.

Remote monitoring of cardiac patients through AI-enabled devices allows for continuous assessment, timely diagnosis, and intervention, significantly improving patient management and outcomes. AI also guides physicians during minimally invasive surgical procedures, enhancing precision and reducing recovery times (Georgiou, 2020).

The Pros and Cons of AI in Healthcare

+ Pros:

- **Enhanced Accuracy and Efficiency**: AI improves diagnostic accuracy and speeds up the treatment planning process, leading to better patient outcomes.
- **Personalized Medicine**: AI enables tailored treatment plans based on individual patient data, moving healthcare towards more personalized approaches.
- **Operational Improvements**: From streamlining patient flow to predictive maintenance of medical equipment, AI optimizes hospital operations, improving service delivery and reducing costs.

– Cons:

- **Data Privacy Concerns**: The reliance on vast datasets raises concerns about patient privacy and the security of sensitive medical information.
- **Risk of Bias**: AI algorithms can inherit biases present in their training data, potentially leading to disparities in patient care.
- **High Implementation Costs**: The initial cost of integrating AI technologies can be prohibitive for some healthcare facilities, especially in low-resource settings.

To sum up, the integration of AI into healthcare is revolutionary, providing unparalleled advancements in diagnostics, treatment planning, and operational efficiency. While challenges remain, particularly around data privacy, bias, and implementation costs, the potential benefits of AI in enhancing patient care and streamlining healthcare operations are immense. As technology evolves, so too will the capabilities of AI in healthcare, promising a future where medical care is more accurate, personalized, and accessible.

AI IN EDUCATION: DEEPENING PERSONALIZATION IN LEARNING

The educational sphere takes a significant leap forward with the incorporation of AI, enabling personalized and optimized learning. From the early use of AI to digitize educational resources to its current role in customizing learning experiences and enhancing educational methodologies, AI's journey in education mirrors its transformative impact across various sectors. AI in education uses intelligent algorithms to analyze learning patterns, adapt to student needs, and provide actionable insights to educators. This revolutionizes traditional teaching and learning paradigms by creating a personalized journey for each student. The shift from static educational content to dynamic, AI-driven learning experiences promotes more engaging, effective, and inclusive educational practices.

One of AI's most significant impacts in education is the personalization of learning. AI systems analyze individual learning patterns, preferences, and performance to tailor content, pace, and learning strategies. This ensures that each student learns in the most effective manner. AI personalizes learning by creating adaptive paths that target gaps in understanding, leading to increased student engagement and success.

Education also benefits from AI through intelligent tutoring systems and collaborative learning environments. These tools not only support traditional learning but also introduce innovative approaches, such as gamified learning experiences that increase student motivation and participation. Additionally, AI's predictive capabilities enable educators to forecast learning outcomes based on real-time data, allowing for timely interventions to support students at risk of falling behind. This proactive approach ensures that all students receive the necessary support to achieve their full potential.

AI technologies also provide unprecedented support for students with special needs. They offer customized learning aids and interfaces designed to overcome specific challenges, from speech recognition software that aids in communication to AI-powered tools that adapt learning materials to various learning disabilities. This fosters an inclusive learning environment where every student can thrive.

Beyond the classroom, AI streamlines administrative tasks, from grading to scheduling. This frees up educators to focus more on teaching and less on paperwork. AI-driven platforms can automate routine administrative duties, optimize resource allocation, and even assist in curriculum design, reflecting AI's comprehensive potential to enhance both teaching and operational efficiencies within educational institutions (Shamkina, 2023).

Pros and Cons of AI in Education

+ Pros:

- **Enhanced Personalization:** AI tailors learning experiences to individual student needs, improving engagement and outcomes.
- **Inclusive Education:** AI provides tools and resources that support special needs education, promoting inclusivity.
- **Efficiency and Support:** By automating administrative tasks and offering real-time feedback, AI allows educators to dedicate more time to teaching and personal interaction with students.

— Cons:

- **Data Privacy and Security:** The use of AI in education raises concerns about the handling and protection of student data.
- **Dependency and Diminished Human Interaction:** There's a risk that reliance on AI tools could reduce valuable face-to-face interactions between teachers and students.
- **Equity and Access:** The implementation of AI in education requires significant investment, potentially exacerbating educational inequalities in under-resourced settings.

Integrating AI into the educational landscape heralds a new era of enhanced learning, efficiency, and inclusivity. Despite the challenges, including data privacy, reduced human interaction, and equity concerns, the potential benefits of AI in transforming education are immense. As AI technologies continue to evolve, their role in education will expand, promising a future where learning is more personalized, accessible, and effective for all students.

Cybersecurity and AI: Fortifying Digital Defenses

The fusion of AI and cybersecurity represents a pivotal evolution in the fight against digital threats. From its inception, AI in cybersecurity has transitioned from a theoretical enhancement to a critical component in detecting, preventing, and responding to cyber threats. This integration has transformed cybersecurity strategies, making them more proactive, intelligent, and capable of defending against increasingly sophisticated attacks.

At first, it was all about automating simple security tasks and analyzing logs for any weird stuff. However, as AI technologies advanced, their role expanded to encompass a wide range of defensive mechanisms, including real-time threat detection, breach risk prediction, and the automation of complex security operations. Today, AI stands as a cornerstone of modern cybersecurity efforts, providing the agility and intelligence necessary to counteract evolving cyber threats.

ENHANCING CYBERSECURITY WITH AI

This technological vanguard enhances the cybersecurity landscape through a multifaceted approach, intertwining threat identification and prevention, breach risk prediction, automated security operations, knowledge consolidation, and advanced vulnerability assessment to create a more resilient digital fortress.

AI's unmatched capability in threat identification and prevention is at the core of its contribution to cybersecurity. By harnessing the power of machine learning algorithms, cybersecurity systems become adept learners, gleaning invaluable insights from historical attack data. This enables them to identify patterns and anomalies indicative of malicious activity, paving the way for the early detection of imminent threats, including the elusive zero-day exploits. Such predictive prowess ensures that vulnerabilities can be addressed proactively, fortifying systems against potential breaches before they occur.

AI-driven systems excel in the art of breach risk prediction by meticulously analyzing network behaviors and detecting anomalies. This continuous surveillance of network traffic, coupled with a keen observation of user behaviors and system vulnerabilities, equips security teams with actionable insights. Armed with this knowledge, they can preemptively bolster their defenses, effectively neutralizing threats before they materialize.

The automation of security operations through AI marks a significant leap in operational efficiency within cybersecurity realms. By taking over routine tasks such as patch management, incident response, and the triage of security alerts, AI liberates cybersecurity professionals to dedicate their focus to strategic challenges. This not only enhances the speed and consistency of responses to potential threats but also optimizes resource allocation within security teams.

AI's role extends beyond immediate threat management to encompass the consolidation of cybersecurity knowledge. By aggregating and analyzing information from a plethora of sources, AI systems foster a comprehensive understanding of the threat landscape. This holistic view aids in informed decision-making and the formulation of robust security strategies, ensuring that defenses are not just reactive but also strategic and well-informed.

I cannot emphasize enough the importance of AI in conducting exhaustive vulnerability assessments and implementing advanced risk mitigation strategies. These systems diligently scan networks for vulnerabilities, prioritizing them based on potential impact and proactively suggesting or even implementing measures to mitigate these risks. This not only enhances the overall security posture but also introduces a level of preemptive defense that is critical in today's cybersecurity landscape.

The efficacy of AI in enhancing cybersecurity is not merely theoretical but is underscored by many applications. AI-powered Security Information and Event Management (SIEM) systems and AI-driven Endpoint Protection Platforms (EPP) are testament to this, playing pivotal roles in detecting unusual network patterns and neutralizing malware in real-time, respectively. These practical implementations highlight AI's indispensable role in safeguarding digital assets against sophisticated threats, showcasing the tangible benefits of integrating AI into cybersecurity strategies.

The Pros and Cons of AI in Cybersecurity

+ Pros:

- **Enhanced Detection and Response:** AI's ability to analyze vast amounts of data in real-time significantly improves the detection of and response to cyber threats.
- **Proactive Threat Prevention:** By predicting potential security breaches, AI enables organizations to adopt a more proactive approach to cybersecurity.
- **Operational Efficiency:** Automation of routine tasks reduces the workload on security teams, allowing them to concentrate on more complex challenges.

— **Cons:**

- **Complexity and Cost:** The implementation of AI in cybersecurity can be complex and costly, potentially limiting access for smaller organizations.
- **False Positives:** While AI enhances threat detection, it can also lead to false positives, requiring careful management to avoid unnecessary alarm.
- **Evolving Threats:** As AI becomes more prevalent in cybersecurity, attackers are also leveraging AI to develop more sophisticated attack methods, creating an ongoing arms race between defenders and attackers.

In a nutshell, AI has revolutionized cybersecurity by changing how we handle digital threats. While challenges such as the complexity of AI systems, the risk of false positives, and the continuous evolution of cyber threats exist, the benefits of AI in enhancing cybersecurity defenses are undeniable. As AI gets better, it'll play a bigger role in cybersecurity. Imagine a future where our digital defenses are just as smart as the threats they're up against.

AI IN CREATIVE INDUSTRIES: BRIDGING TECHNOLOGY AND ARTISTRY

The combination of AI and creative industries represents a major shift in the conception, creation, and consumption of art, literature, music, and design. AI's foray into these realms has not only expanded the horizons of creativity but also introduced a new paradigm where technology and human ingenuity intersect, offering both unprecedented opportunities and unique challenges.

Unleashing Creativity Across Domains

The role of AI in creative fields is both diverse and transformative, spanning across graphic design, content creation, advertising, marketing, and more.

- **Graphic Design and Content Creation:** AI tools have revolutionized graphic design and content creation, automating tasks like image editing and layout design and generating creative content ideas. These technologies enable designers to experiment with novel aesthetics and styles, pushing the boundaries of traditional design.
- **Advertising and Marketing:** In advertising, AI's data-driven insights help tailor marketing campaigns to specific audiences, enhancing engagement through personalized content. AI algorithms analyze consumer behavior to predict trends, enabling marketers to craft strategies that resonate deeply with their target demographics.
- **Film and Video Production:** The film industry benefits from AI in streamlining production processes, from script analysis to visual effects and post-production editing. AI applications can simulate realistic environments, automate editing tasks, and even predict audience preferences, facilitating more efficient and targeted storytelling.
- **Fashion Design:** AI in fashion design offers a blend of trend forecasting and personalized design

recommendations. By analyzing current trends and historical data, AI assists designers in creating innovative fashion lines that appeal to contemporary tastes while optimizing supply chains for sustainability and efficiency.

- **Music Composition:** AI's impact on music composition is profound, enabling the creation of new compositions by analyzing patterns in music theory and existing works. Tools like AIVA compose original music that spans genres, demonstrating AI's potential as a creative collaborator.
- **Architecture and Design:** In architecture, AI aids in optimizing building designs for efficiency, sustainability, and aesthetics. Algorithms generate design alternatives based on specific criteria, allowing architects to explore innovative solutions that balance form and function.
- **Writing and Literature:** AI applications in writing and literature range from generating creative writing prompts to assisting in the editing process. AI-powered tools can compose narrative pieces, suggesting new ways to approach storytelling.
- **Gaming and Game Design:** AI transforms gaming through dynamic game environments that adapt to player actions, creating more immersive and personalized gaming experiences. AI designs complex game levels, enhances NPC behavior, and even aids in testing, ensuring engaging and bug-free gameplay.

From Adobe's Sensei, which aids in graphic design tasks, to IBM's Watson, which has been used to create movie trailers and compose music, real-world applications of AI in creative industries abound. These tools not only automate mundane tasks but also provide creative professionals with new avenues for exploration and expression.

Pros and Cons of AI in Creative Industries

+ Pros:

- **Enhanced Creativity and Efficiency:** AI opens new creative possibilities and streamlines production processes, allowing creators more time to focus on innovation.
- **Personalization:** AI enables the creation of personalized content, from marketing materials to interactive gaming experiences, catering to individual preferences.
- **Accessibility:** AI tools make creative expression more accessible, lowering barriers to entry for aspiring artists, musicians, and writers.

— Cons:

- **Authenticity Concerns:** The use of AI in creative processes raises questions about the authenticity and originality of the resulting works.
- **Job Displacement Fears:** There is concern that AI automation could displace jobs in creative fields, though many argue AI acts more as a tool for enhancement rather than replacement.
- **Ethical and Copyright Issues:** AI-generated content presents complex ethical and copyright issues,

challenging existing legal frameworks and raising debates over intellectual property rights.

To put it simply, the integration of AI into creative industries signals a new age of innovation, providing tools that bolster, enhance, and occasionally disrupt traditional creative methods. While the journey of AI in these fields is accompanied by both enthusiasm and apprehension, the potential for AI to inspire new forms of artistic expression and creative solutions is undeniable. As we navigate this evolving landscape, the dialogue between technology and creativity promises to yield a richer, more diverse world of art, design, and storytelling.

AI'S PIONEERING ROLE IN ECONOMIC GROWTH

The advent of AI in the economy heralds a dual-edged revolution, profoundly reshaping job markets, spurring economic growth, and altering societal structures. This integration brings about remarkable efficiencies and innovation while also presenting significant challenges.

AI's multifaceted contribution to economic growth encompasses driving productivity, fostering the emergence of new markets, and enhancing the quality and accessibility of goods and services. By automating routine and labor-intensive tasks, AI liberates the workforce to engage in more complex and innovative endeavors, thus amplifying overall productivity. Moreover, AI's advanced data analysis capabilities empower businesses to streamline operations, minimize waste, and facilitate informed decision-making, further fueling economic efficiency.

This technological evolution has catalyzed the creation of entirely new industries and markets, such as AI-enhanced healthcare solutions, autonomous vehicles, and AI-powered financial advisory services. These innovations not only stimulate economic growth but also significantly improve societal well-being by making services more accessible and enhancing the convenience of daily life.

The transformative impact of AI extends deeply into the job market, sparking extensive debate. While AI's automation capabilities threaten to displace traditional roles in sectors like manufacturing and customer service, they also herald the creation of new opportunities in AI development and oversight, as well as sectors poised to benefit from AI-driven productivity enhancements.

AI's real-world applications illustrate its profound economic and societal impact. In healthcare, machine learning models are revolutionizing diagnostics, enabling quicker and more accurate disease identification, thus saving lives and reducing costs by diminishing the reliance on expensive diagnostic procedures. In the financial realm, AI algorithms that analyze market trends and manage investments are democratizing financial advice, thereby improving investment outcomes for a broader segment of the population.

The creative industries, too, have been transformed by AI, with technologies enabling graphic designers, musicians, and writers to push the boundaries of creativity. This not only fosters the growth of the creative economy but also enhances the accessibility of cultural products, enriching the societal landscape.

Simultaneously, AI is anticipated to augment existing jobs, providing tools that boost worker efficiency and foster innovation. For instance, AI assists doctors in more accurately diagnosing diseases, aids architects in designing safer buildings, and enables personalized education experiences, showcasing the technology's potential to enrich professional practices across various fields.

The integration of AI brings about unprecedented economic growth and societal benefits by enhancing productivity, creating new markets, and improving the quality of life. Yet, it also needs to navigate the challenges of job displacement, market transformation, and the ethical implications of widespread automation. As we move forward, the continued evolution of AI promises to further redefine the economic and societal landscape, emphasizing the need for adaptive strategies to harness its full potential while mitigating its challenges.

Pros and Cons of AI in the Economy

+ Pros:

- **Increased Productivity and Efficiency:** AI automates routine tasks, allowing humans to focus on higher-value work, thereby boosting productivity and economic growth.
- **Innovation and New Market Creation:** AI drives innovation, leading to the development of new products, services, and markets.
- **Enhanced Quality of Life:** AI applications in healthcare, transportation, and other sectors

improve accessibility and convenience, enhancing societal well-being.

– **Cons:**

- **Job Displacement:** While AI creates new jobs, it also automates existing ones, leading to concerns about job displacement and the need for workforce retraining.
- **Inequality:** The benefits of AI-driven economic growth could be unevenly distributed, exacerbating income inequality if proactive measures are not taken.
- **Dependency and Security Risks:** Increased reliance on AI systems introduces new vulnerabilities, including the risk of AI-driven systems being compromised.

AI's role in the economy is a catalyst for growth, innovation, and societal progress. However, navigating its challenges—such as job displacement, inequality, and security risks—requires thoughtful policies and frameworks to ensure that the benefits of AI are broadly shared and its risks are mitigated. As we continue to integrate AI into various economic sectors, the focus must remain on harnessing its potential while fostering an inclusive and resilient economic future.

AI UNLEASHED: TRANSFORMING INDUSTRIES AND SHAPING THE FUTURE

Exploring the vast applications of AI takes us on a transformative journey through healthcare, education, cybersecurity, creative industries, and the global economy. Here, I aim to showcase the transformative power of AI, summarize its profound impacts, explore real-world applications, and open up a discussion on advanced AI technologies shaping our world.

AI in Healthcare: The Lifesaver in the Digital Age

AI stands as a sentinel in healthcare, wielding the dual swords of precision and efficiency to combat disease and save lives. It's not just a tool but a partner that empowers healthcare professionals with deep insights for early disease detection, personalized treatment strategies, and streamlined administrative workflows. Imagine a world where every diagnosis is accurate, every treatment is tailored, and every administrative task is automated—this is the promise of AI in healthcare, a promise of a healthier future for all.

AI in Education: The Architect of Personalized Learning

In the realm of education, AI emerges as the architect of personalized learning experiences, constructing pathways of knowledge that adapt to the unique journey of each learner. It democratizes education, making learning accessible, engaging, and effective. Through AI, educational content evolves in real time, responding to the needs of students and empowering educators to unlock the full potential of every mind. This is the classroom of the future—dynamic, inclusive, and inspired by AI.

AI in Cybersecurity: The Guardian of the Digital Frontier

As the guardian of our digital frontiers, AI stands vigilant against the specters of cyber threats. It transforms cybersecurity from a reactive defense to a proactive shield, employing advanced algorithms to predict, detect, and neutralize threats before they can breach our digital lives. AI in cybersecurity is not just about protecting data; it's about safeguarding our way of life in an increasingly connected world.

AI in Creative Industries: The Muse of the Digital Renaissance

AI in creative industries is the muse of a digital renaissance, igniting the sparks of creativity and innovation. It redefines art, music, literature, and design, enabling creators to explore uncharted territories of expression. From generating novel artworks to composing symphonies and penning stories, AI collaborates with human creativity to produce works that resonate with our deepest emotions and aspirations. This is the dawn of a new era in creativity, illuminated by AI.

AI in the Economy: The Engine of Growth and Innovation

AI fuels the engine of economic growth and innovation, driving productivity, spawning new markets, and enhancing the quality of life. It reshapes job markets, fosters sustainable development, and paves the way for prosperity in an interconnected world. The economic impact of AI is a narrative of transformation—where efficiency meets opportunity and innovation heralds growth. This is the economy of the future, powered by AI.

As we stand on the precipice of a new chapter in the saga of AI, we look back at the journey traversed—a journey of transformation across healthcare, education, cybersecurity, creative industries, and the economy. AI's potential to revolutionize industries and elevate societal well-being shines brightly as a beacon of hope and innovation.

With each application, AI weaves a richer narrative of human achievement, setting the stage for the exploration of advanced AI technologies that lie ahead. This chapter not only documents the impact of AI but also establishes the groundwork for comprehending the significant advancements that are shaping our world. As we transition to the exploration of advanced AI technologies globally, the anticipation for uncovering the next frontier of AI's possibilities grows, promising a future where AI and human potential converge to redefine what it means to live, work, and thrive in the digital age.

UNLOCKING THE REVOLUTION

"Knowledge is power."

— FRANCIS BACON

AI is the future… and it's already upon us. It's already playing a far greater role than many people realize, yet it's shrouded in a fear of the unknown. You're reading this because you knew it was important to build your understanding of AI – and you were correct. It isn't going anywhere, and if we don't make an effort to understand it and overcome the barriers that stand in our way, we're going to be left behind as the future unfolds.

Navigating the AI landscape requires confidence and the foundational understanding necessary to be secure in our knowledge that it isn't something to fear. AI is a reliable tool we can use to help us overcome challenges and unlock opportunities that would otherwise be inaccessible – and increasingly, our world is going to demand that we know how to use it. My mission is to make sure that as many people as possible are confident with using AI so that they're ready for what's to come.

One thing AI can't do, however, is help more people find this key to unlocking their understanding, so it's at this stage in our journey that I'm compelled to ask for your help.

By leaving a review of this book on Amazon, you'll show new readers where they can find the route to this essential understanding and make sure they're not left behind by the revolution.

There's no shortage of people looking up AI, but there's a lot of noise out there. Your review will help them to find the understanding they're looking for and discover what AI is really capable of.

Thank you so much for your support. This is more important than many people realize, and I'm grateful for your help in spreading this information.

5

ADVANCED AI TECHNOLOGIES AND INDUSTRY GIANTS

> *In our business, we talk about emerging technologies and how they impact society. We've never seen a technology move as fast as AI has to impact society and technology. This is by far the fastest moving tech-*

nology that we've ever tracked in terms of its impact and we're just getting started.

— PAUL DAUGHERTY

The dawn of AI represents not just an evolution but a revolution in the technological landscape, transforming every sector it touches and redefining the boundaries of what is possible. The pace of AI technology advancement, as noted by Paul Daugherty, has had an unprecedented influence on society, the economy, and individual lives. This rapid evolution is not the work of a single entity but the result of contributions from myriad key players in the AI industry, each driving forward the frontier of AI capabilities.

I intend to remove the mystery surrounding the current state of AI technologies and platforms in this chapter, presenting a panoramic view of worldwide AI progress. In our exploration of the AI ecosystem, we uncover the innovations shaping future advancements and the industry giants who are leading the way.

The journey through this chapter will reveal how these key players—ranging from established tech giants to dynamic startups—are not only pushing the limits of AI's technological capabilities but also influencing how society engages with and understands AI. From healthcare to education, cybersecurity to creative industries, the impact of AI is profound and pervasive, reflecting a technological evolution that is unparalleled in both scope and speed.

While navigating AI technologies, we discover innovations that will shape our future, emphasizing the significance of understanding AI's trajectory for all individuals interested in society and technology. This chapter serves as a gateway to comprehending the vast, intricate world of AI, illuminating the path AI is carving in the digital age and its implications for the future.

AI'S INFLUENCE ON GLOBAL TECH TRENDS

In the landscape of global technology trends, AI is emerging as a transformative force, redefining the realms of innovation, efficiency, and strategic foresight. As we venture deeper into this transformative era, it's imperative to grasp how AI is not merely influencing but actively sculpting these trends across various domains. It is essential to comprehend this as we move forward into a future where AI seamlessly integrates into our lives, demanding a reassessment of our readiness and acceptance of this technology.

Cognitive Computing and Predictive Analytics: A New Paradigm

Central to AI's transformative capacity is its proficiency in leveraging cognitive computing and predictive analytics to distill actionable insights from extensive and intricate datasets. This capability is revolutionizing decision-making processes, from personal choices to organizational strategies, by enabling the identification of patterns and forecasting future trends with remarkable precision. Such advancements not only propel innovation but also refine the efficiency of decision-making models, facilitating a more nimble adaptation to evolving market conditions.

The breadth of AI's impact is extensive. In healthcare, for instance, predictive analytics can anticipate outbreaks, enhancing readiness and response measures. In the finance sector, cognitive computing aids in more precise risk evaluations, leading to informed investment decisions. The capacity of AI to drive progress and mitigate risks across industries is vast, highlighting its role as a crucial driver in shaping global technology trends (*Immersive Technologies for Education*, n.d.).

The Rise of Autonomous Systems

The proliferation of autonomous systems signifies another critical trend driven by AI. These systems, from self-driving vehicles to automated manufacturing processes, underscore a move towards more intelligent, self-managing technologies capable of functioning with minimal human oversight. The enhancement of efficiency and safety in sectors like transportation, manufacturing, and urban planning through AI integration into autonomous systems heralds a revolution, redefining standards of productivity and reimagining the essence of work and mobility (Banafa, 2024).

Driving Innovation and Informed Decision-Making Models

The influence of AI in fostering innovation and informed decision-making models is profound. AI's ability to synthesize data from varied sources to understand complex issues is pivotal for innovation, laying the groundwork for new products, services, and technologies that cater to emerging demands and preferences.

Additionally, AI's predictive capabilities are key in the process of decision-making. By accurately projecting trends and outcomes, AI empowers organizations to make choices that are strategically aligned and responsive to future market dynamics.

In an ever-evolving technological landscape, it is indispensable to take a proactive stance in decision-making. This proactive approach becomes even more crucial as success is defined by anticipating and adapting to future challenges (K, 2023). It is important to acknowledge the significant impact of AI on global technology trends, which can be seen through cognitive computing, predictive analytics, and the emergence of autonomous systems. With this in mind, the forthcoming discussion will focus on how individuals, businesses, and communities can effectively prepare for and embrace this transformative technology.

The seamless integration of AI into our daily routines and operational frameworks presents a spectrum of opportunities and challenges, calling for a strategic adoption approach that thoughtfully addresses ethical, social, and economic ramifications.

The following section will examine practical strategies and tactics for facilitating a seamless transition to a future with AI augmentation. This encompasses cultivating an AI-ready culture, upskilling and reskilling the workforce, and employing AI towards sustainable development goals (Theodotou, 2023). By adopting a comprehensive and forward-looking approach, we can leverage AI's potential not just for technological advancement but also for enhancing societal well-being, paving the way for a future where technology and humanity coalesce in harmony (Spataro, 2023).

PREPARATION AND EMBRACE OF AI

In an era where AI is reshaping the contours of our global technological landscape, the imperative for individuals, businesses, and communities to adapt and embrace this transformation is pronounced. AI's evolution brings forth an array of challenges and opportunities, requiring a concerted effort toward readiness and integration. This readiness hinges on three pivotal strategies: upskilling, fostering a lifelong learning culture, and promoting human-AI collaboration. Each of these strategies plays a vital role in leveraging AI's capabilities to augment human potential and drive societal advancement.

Upskilling: Bridging the AI Skills Gap

At the heart of adapting to AI is upskilling—the process of teaching current employees, individuals, and community members new, relevant skills. This endeavor is crucial in a landscape where AI technologies demand a workforce proficient in digital skills and literate in AI applications. For individuals, this means embarking on a journey of learning and mastery in areas such as data analysis, machine learning, and AI integration, which are not only vital for personal growth but also for ensuring employability in an AI-dominated future.

Businesses, in response, must anchor their strategic planning in robust training programs that arm their employees with the knowledge and tools to work alongside AI technologies seamlessly. The significance of upskilling transcends the mere acquisition of new skills—it cultivates a workforce that is resilient, adaptable, and prepared for the future, thereby enhancing job satisfaction, productivity, and fostering a culture of continuous improvement (eLearning Industry, n.d.).

Promoting a Lifelong Learning Culture

The velocity of AI's evolution necessitates a shift in perspective towards education and learning. In this new paradigm, learning becomes a lifelong endeavor—a continuous pursuit of knowledge and skills in response to an ever-evolving technological milieu. For individuals, adopting a mindset characterized by curiosity and an unwavering commitment to learning is indispensable. This approach ensures staying abreast of the latest advancements in AI and related fields, positioning oneself favorably in a dynamic environment.

On the organizational level, cultivating a lifelong learning culture is pivotal. This can be achieved through facilitating access to a spectrum of learning opportunities, including online courses, workshops, and seminars, alongside promoting mentorship and knowledge-sharing initiatives. By cultivating such a culture, individuals and communities can effectively navigate the AI-driven landscape and nurture human ingenuity and creativity (HBR, 2023).

Emphasizing Human-AI Collaboration

The integration of AI into daily operations heralds a new era of collaboration between humans and machines. This collaborative synergy capitalizes on the strengths of both—combining human creativity, empathy, and strategic insight with AI's computational speed, accuracy, and efficiency. The essence of maximizing this collaboration lies in designing AI systems that complement rather than supplant human roles, thereby augmenting human capabilities and enhancing decision-making processes.

For businesses and communities, fostering an environment that promotes interdisciplinary teamwork—where AI experts and professionals from various fields converge to tackle complex challenges—is essential. Such collaboration not only paves the way for innovative solutions but also deepens our understanding of AI's ethical and effective application in society (Javinpaul, 2023).

In this AI-driven era, upskilling, lifelong learning, and human-AI collaboration are vital for thriving in a transformed landscape. These strategies ensure not only the adaptability and competitiveness of individuals, businesses, and communities but also the ethical and beneficial integration of AI into the fabric of society, enriching human potential and driving progress in an increasingly interconnected world.

LEADING NATIONS IN THE AI RACE

Different countries are making significant strides in AI research and technology, contributing to a global race towards technological supremacy. This section will explore the leading countries in the AI arena, highlighting their key advancements and contributions to the field. By understanding these global efforts, we can appreciate the diverse approaches to AI development and the collaborative potential that exists worldwide.

The international competition in AI research and development is a testament to the technology's transformative potential across various sectors. Countries are investing heavily in AI to gain a competitive edge, foster economic growth, and address societal challenges. According to InvestGlass (2023), the United States and China are at the forefront of the AI race, with countries like Canada, Japan, the United Kingdom, South Korea, France, India, Germany, and Singapore also making notable contributions (Keary, 2024).

United States: A Cradle of AI Innovation

The United States is often seen as the birthplace of AI, with its roots deeply embedded in the research labs of MIT, Stanford, and other prestigious universities. This rich history has evolved into a vibrant ecosystem of innovation fueled by leading tech giants such as Google, Apple, and Facebook, as well as a thriving startup scene that continues to push the boundaries of AI technology.

Driving Forces Behind the US AI Boom

- **Research and Development (R&D)**: The US government's investment in AI research, through initiatives like the National AI Research and Development Strategic Plan, has laid a solid foundation for growth. This is complemented by private sector investments from companies like Amazon, which spent $22.6 billion on R&D in 2017 alone.
- **Talent and Education**: Home to some of the world's leading universities offering specialized AI programs, the US has become a magnet for global AI talent. This educational prowess not only fuels the country's AI development but also fosters a culture of innovation and entrepreneurship.
- **Regulatory Environment**: The US approach to AI regulation has been relatively hands-off, promoting a favorable environment for technological experimentation and rapid commercialization.

Key Achievements and Innovations

- **AI in Healthcare**: American companies are at the forefront of using AI in healthcare, with innovations like IBM Watson's ability to analyze medical data and provide insights into patient care.
- **Autonomous Vehicles**: U.S.-based Tesla and Waymo are leading the race in developing self-driving technology, with significant advancements in autonomous navigation and safety systems.

- **AI Ethics and Governance**: Recognizing the ethical implications of AI, institutions like the AI Now Institute at New York University are pioneering research into AI's social impacts, setting a global benchmark for responsible AI development.

China: Ambitious Plans and Rapid Progress

China's government has declared AI development a national priority, with an ambitious goal to become the world leader in AI by 2030. This state-driven approach is supported by massive investments, a vast data pool, and a strategic focus on AI applications across various sectors.

Strategic Investments and Government Support

- **National AI Development Plan**: Announced in 2017, this plan outlines China's strategy to dominate AI globally, with specific targets for the country's AI industry's value and capabilities by 2030.
- **Data Advantage**: With the world's largest internet user base, Chinese companies have access to unparalleled data volumes, facilitating the training and refinement of AI algorithms.
- **Focus on Education**: China is snowballing its AI education programs, aiming to cultivate a new generation of AI experts and researchers to drive future innovations.

Breakthroughs and Areas of Dominance

- **Facial Recognition Technology**: Chinese companies like Megvii and SenseTime are leading in facial recognition technology, with applications ranging from security to financial services.
- **Smart Cities**: Leveraging AI, China is transforming urban management and services, exemplified by projects like Alibaba's "City Brain" in Hangzhou, which optimizes traffic flow and public services using AI.
- **Global AI Influence**: Beyond domestic achievements, Chinese AI companies are expanding globally, investing in AI startups worldwide, and exporting AI technologies, thereby extending China's influence in the global AI landscape.

Canada: A Hub for AI Research

Canada is recognized globally for its foundational contributions to AI, particularly in deep learning. The country's strategy focuses on research excellence and ethical AI development, supported by both the public and private sectors.

Foundations of Excellence

- **Academic Leadership**: Canada boasts pioneers in AI research, such as Geoffrey Hinton, Yoshua Bengio, and Richard Sutton, whose work laid the groundwork for modern AI technologies.
- **Government Support**: The Pan-Canadian Artificial Intelligence Strategy aims to strengthen Canada's

position as a leading destination for AI research, emphasizing ethical AI development and public engagement.

Noteworthy Contributions

- **AI in Health Care**: Projects like the AI-powered BlueDot, which first identified the risk from COVID-19, highlight Canada's role in using AI for global health.
- **Ethical AI Frameworks**: Canada is at the forefront of developing ethical guidelines for AI, emphasizing accountability and social impact through initiatives like the Montreal Declaration for Responsible AI.

Japan: Pioneering AI in Robotics and Society

Japan's approach to AI integrates technological advancement with societal needs, particularly focusing on its aging population and labor shortages.

Technological Integration and Societal Solutions

- **Robotics**: Japan's advancements in robotics, often powered by AI, are world-renowned, with applications in manufacturing, healthcare, and personal assistance.
- **Government Initiatives**: The Japanese government's "Society 5.0" initiative envisions integrating digital technologies, including AI, into every aspect of life to solve societal challenges.

Achievements and Innovations

- **Automation in Elderly Care**: Companies like Toyota are developing robotic assistants to support the elderly, showcasing the blend of AI with compassionate care.
- **Disaster Prediction and Management**: AI technologies are employed to predict natural disasters and manage emergency responses, which is critical for Japan's disaster-prone areas.

United Kingdom: Leading in Ethical AI Development

The UK's AI strategy is distinguished by its focus on ethical development and leveraging AI for the public good, supported by a robust academic and startup ecosystem.

Ethical Leadership and Innovation

- **Academic Excellence**: The UK's universities are integral to its AI ecosystem, producing cutting-edge research and talent.
- **AI for Good**: The UK government's emphasis on using AI to address societal challenges is evident in its support for projects in healthcare, environmental protection, and education.

Key Developments

- **NHS and AI**: The National Health Service (NHS) in the UK is exploring AI to improve patient care and operational efficiency, setting an example of AI's potential in public health.

- **AI in Financial Services**: London's position as a global financial center has spurred innovations in AI for finance, with startups and established firms alike adopting AI for everything from fraud detection to personalized customer services.

South Korea: A Tech-Driven AI Vision

South Korea's commitment to AI is part of its broader vision to lead in technological innovation, with significant investments in AI research and development aimed at enhancing its economic and societal capabilities.

Strategic Investments in AI

- **Government Funding**: South Korea has announced substantial investments in AI, aiming to secure a leading position in the global AI market by fostering innovation and talent.
- **Corporate Leadership**: Global tech giants like Samsung and LG are heavily investing in AI, applying it across consumer electronics, semiconductors, and telecommunications.

AI Achievements

- **AI in Manufacturing**: South Korea is utilizing AI to maintain its leadership in manufacturing, especially in electronics and automobiles, through smart factories and automation.

- **Education and Research**: The establishment of AI research centers and universities dedicated to AI is set to nurture future talent and innovation.

France: Championing Ethical AI

France's approach to AI emphasizes ethical considerations and societal benefits, aiming to make France a leader in trustworthy AI on the European stage.

Ethical AI Development

- **AI for Humanity**: France has launched initiatives like AI for Humanity, which stress the importance of developing AI in an ethical, transparent, and accountable manner.
- **Public Investment**: The French government has pledged significant funding for AI research, focusing on areas such as healthcare, transportation, and environmental sustainability.

Contributions to AI

- **AI Research Hubs**: Paris is becoming a prominent center for AI research, with collaborations between academic institutions, startups, and major corporations.
- **Global AI Forum**: France has taken the lead in organizing global discussions on AI governance and ethics, highlighting its commitment to responsible AI development.

India: Focusing on AI for Social Good

India's AI strategy is uniquely focused on applying AI to address social challenges, leveraging its robust IT industry and startup ecosystem to develop inclusive AI technologies.

AI for Inclusive Growth

- **National AI Strategy**: India aims to leverage AI for inclusive economic growth, addressing challenges in healthcare, education, and agriculture.
- **Startup Innovation**: The vibrant startup scene in India is actively exploring AI solutions tailored to local needs and challenges, supported by government initiatives.

Notable Initiatives

- **AI in Healthcare**: Indian startups are using AI to improve access to healthcare services and diagnostics in rural areas.
- **Skill Development**: Programs aimed at training the youth in AI and digital technologies are set to enhance India's talent pool.

Germany: Engineering AI Excellence

Germany's AI strategy integrates its engineering prowess with AI innovation, focusing on enhancing its manufacturing sector and addressing societal challenges.

Manufacturing and AI

- **Industry 4.0**: Germany is a pioneer of the Industry 4.0 movement, integrating AI with manufacturing to create smart factories that boost efficiency and innovation.
- **Research and Collaboration**: The German government supports AI research through funding and partnerships between academia and industry.

AI Applications

- **Automotive AI**: German automotive companies are leaders in incorporating AI into autonomous driving technologies and smart manufacturing processes.
- **Ethical AI Frameworks**: Germany advocates for stringent ethical standards in AI development, emphasizing the importance of transparency and accountability.

Singapore: A Smart Nation Powered by AI

Singapore's AI strategy is an integral part of its Smart Nation vision, aiming to utilize AI to enhance public services, healthcare, and urban living.

Strategic AI Integration

- **Government-Led Initiatives**: The Singaporean government is actively promoting AI adoption in key sectors, including healthcare, finance, and urban solutions, through funding and policy support.

- **Collaborative Ecosystem**: Singapore fosters a collaborative AI ecosystem, bringing together research institutions, startups, and corporations to innovate and apply AI solutions.

AI Highlights

- **AI in Healthcare**: Projects like AI-powered diagnostic tools are improving healthcare outcomes and efficiency.
- **Urban Solutions**: AI is being used to enhance public transportation, urban planning, and sustainability efforts, making Singapore a model for smart cities globally.

Each of these countries illustrates the diverse approaches and strategic priorities that shape the global AI landscape. From South Korea's tech-driven vision to Germany's engineering excellence and from India's focus on AI for social good to Singapore's smart nation initiatives, the global pursuit of AI innovation is a testament to the technology's transformative potential across societal and economic dimensions.

Understanding AI Platforms

AI platforms are comprehensive environments designed to facilitate the development, deployment, and scaling of artificial intelligence applications. These platforms typically offer a suite of tools that help process vast amounts of data, develop machine learning models, and integrate AI into various applications. By providing essential resources such as computational power, data storage, and pre-built algorithms, AI platforms help to accelerate the adoption and innovation of AI technologies across industries.

To navigate the diverse landscape of AI platforms, let's compare several leading platforms, highlighting their distinct features, strengths, and areas where they may fall short.

Google AI Platform

- **Strengths**: Google's platform excels in scalability and integrates advanced machine learning models, benefiting from Google's extensive data resources (predictiveanalyticstoday.com).
- **Weaknesses**: Complexity and potentially high costs for extensive use are notable drawbacks.

TensorFlow

- **Strengths**: As an open-source framework, TensorFlow is renowned for its flexibility, strong community support, and suitability for deep learning projects.
- **Weaknesses**: Its comprehensive nature introduces a steep learning curve, making it daunting for beginners.

Microsoft Azure

- **Strengths**: Azure stands out for its wide array of cognitive services and enterprise-grade security,

offering robust solutions for integrating AI functionalities into applications.
- **Weaknesses**: The platform's extensive service offerings can be overwhelming, with costs scaling significantly with usage.

Rainbird

- **Strengths**: Specializing in automating decision-making, Rainbird is distinguished by its ability to model complex decision trees and provide explainable AI outputs.
- **Weaknesses**: Its niche focus limits its applicability across broader AI application domains.

Infosys Nia

- **Strengths**: Infosys Nia integrates machine learning with big data analytics and knowledge management, tailored for enhancing business processes in enterprise environments.
- **Weaknesses**: The platform's enterprise orientation may not be as accessible for smaller teams or projects.

SELECTING THE RIGHT AI PLATFORM

Selecting the right AI platform is a critical decision that hinges on a deep understanding of each platform's unique capabilities, strengths, and limitations. In the rapidly evolving landscape of artificial intelligence, platforms like Google AI Platform, TensorFlow, Microsoft Azure, and others offer diverse tools and environments tailored to specific AI development needs. Google's AI Platform is celebrated for its scalability and advanced machine learning models, drawing on Google's extensive data and computing resources. However, its complexity and potential cost can be daunting for some users. TensorFlow, an open-source framework developed by Google, is favored for its flexibility and robust support in deep learning projects despite a steep learning curve that may challenge newcomers.

Microsoft Azure distinguishes itself with a broad spectrum of cognitive services and enterprise-grade security, providing powerful solutions for integrating AI functionalities into various applications, albeit at a potential cost premium. On the niche end, platforms like Rainbird focus on automated decision-making processes, offering unique value in creating explainable AI outputs but with limited applicability beyond specific decision-making contexts. Similarly, Infosys Nia caters to enterprise needs by merging machine learning, big data analytics, and knowledge management to optimize business processes, though its accessibility and applicability might be constrained for smaller projects or teams.

The selection process should consider several critical factors, including the specific requirements of the AI application, the expertise level of the team, budget constraints, and the need for scalability and integration with existing systems. For instance, startups or projects emphasizing deep learning might gravitate towards TensorFlow for its comprehensive libraries and community support, while larger enterprises requiring robust, secure, and scalable AI solutions might opt for the likes of Microsoft Azure or Google AI Platform.

Conversely, projects needing specialized AI functionalities, such as advanced decision-making or legal analytics, might find their solution in more focused platforms like Rainbird or Premonition.

The ecosystem of AI platforms provides a foundational base for the development and deployment of AI applications, with each platform catering to different facets of AI innovation. As the field continues to evolve, these platforms will undoubtedly play a crucial role in shaping the future of technology and industry.

EMBRACING THE GLOBAL AI MOSAIC: INSIGHTS INTO PLATFORMS AND PROGRESS

I crafted this section to distill and organize the wealth of knowledge we've navigated through in this chapter, offering a concise summary that highlights the essence of global AI advancements and the intricate world of AI platforms. Through these insights, we aim to fortify your understanding of the international AI landscape and the diverse tools that drive its expansion.

Global AI Advancements: A Tapestry of Innovation

The journey into AI's global footprint reveals a rich tapestry of innovation, where countries across continents contribute to the field's evolution with distinct focuses and strategies. From the technological prowess of the United States and China to the ethical AI pursuits of the United Kingdom and France, each nation carves its niche in the AI domain. Canada's emphasis on research, India's focus on AI for social good, and Japan's integration of AI to address demographic challenges exemplify the multifaceted approaches to harnessing AI's potential. This global endeavor not only underscores the universal appeal and applicability of AI but also highlights collaborative opportunities that transcend geographical boundaries.

AI Tools and Platforms: Harnessing Technology for Innovation

The exploration of AI platforms unveils a spectrum of tools designed to democratize access to AI technologies, each with unique strengths and potential limitations. Google AI Platform and Microsoft Azure emerge as comprehensive ecosystems offering a wide range of services and machine learning models, though their complexity and potential costs necessitate careful consideration. TensorFlow stands out for its flexibility in deep learning projects, which is supported by a vibrant open-source community. Specialized platforms like Rainbird and Infosys Nia cater to niche requirements, offering solutions for decision-making automation and enterprise-level integrations, respectively. This overview not only aids in selecting the appropriate platform for specific project needs but also reflects the dynamic nature of AI development tools.

From Global Perspectives to Technological Platforms: A Unified View

The insights garnered from examining AI's international developments and the platforms that underpin technological innovation provide a foundational understanding of the field's current state and future trajectory. As we delve into the practical applications and programming nuances of AI in the upcoming chapter, this consolidated knowledge base serves as a vital reference point. The rapid pace of AI advancements worldwide, coupled with the emergence of sophisticated platforms, signals a transformative era in technology and society.

Chapter Summary and Look Ahead

Through this exploration, we've illuminated the mechanisms driving AI innovation globally and the platforms facilitating its widespread adoption. This narrative not only enriches our appreciation of the international efforts shaping AI but also emphasizes the importance of understanding the diverse tools at our disposal. As we transition to discussing AI's programming aspects and its seamless integration into daily life, the groundwork laid here will enhance our grasp of how AI technologies are being crafted and applied to reshape our world.

Chapter 5 promises to deepen this exploration, focusing on the programming languages and frameworks that bring AI applications to life. This shift from a macroscopic view of AI's global impact to the microscopic intricacies of its creation marks a crucial step in comprehending AI's transformative potential. By bridging theoretical insights with practical applications, we continue our journey through the evolving landscape of artificial intelligence, poised to uncover how it's becoming an indispensable part of our daily lives, making the future of technology not only a distant dream but an immediate reality.

6

PROGRAMMING THE FUTURE: AI DEVELOPMENT AND CODING LANGUAGES

> *Programming is the art of algorithm design and the craft of debugging errant code.*
>
> — ELLEN ULLMAN

Programming is more than just writing lines of code; it is a complex and dynamic field that requires constant learning and adaptation. As we venture into the intricate dance of algorithms and debugging that forms the backbone of AI, we're not just exploring a technical discipline. We're embarking on a journey into the heart of a revolution—a revolution powered by the symbiotic relationship between human creativity and machine intelligence.

At the core of AI's transformative power lies a sophisticated yet intricate interplay between algorithmic design and code refinement. This narrative isn't just about the languages we use to instruct machines but also about the frameworks that make AI development accessible and the impact it has on our lives. It's a story of how these tools and methodologies enable us to push the boundaries of what machines can learn, comprehend, and execute—mirroring and often surpassing human cognitive capabilities.

Working with AI is similar to having a constant back-and-forth discussion between the developer and the machine, refining code, and exchanging information. It's a process of translation, where human intentions are converted into a language that machines can understand and act upon. This dialogue is facilitated by programming languages like Python, revered for its simplicity and readability, making it an ideal choice for AI developers worldwide. The exploration of AI's underpinnings will also take us through the roles played by languages such as R, Java, and C++, each contributing uniquely to the development of AI, from statistical analysis to the construction of elaborate neural networks.

However, the journey doesn't end with the languages. It extends into the realms of frameworks and tools like TensorFlow, PyTorch, and Keras. These are not just technological aids but the very engines of innovation in AI. They democratize AI development, offering a treasure trove of libraries and resources that simplify complex machine learning model implementations. These frameworks are the unsung heroes that empower developers to experiment, iterate, and deploy AI applications with a speed and efficiency that was unimaginable just a decade ago.

Yet, as we delve deeper, we find that the future of AI programming is not just shaped by technological advancements but also by the ethical considerations that guide its development. The narrative will thus weave through the emerging trends that promise to redefine AI's potential, from quantum computing's promise to exponentially increase processing capabilities to the ethical frameworks that ensure AI's development remains responsible and aligned with human values.

This exploration is more than an academic exercise; it's an invitation to engage with AI development hands-on. To learn AI programming is to participate in an ongoing discovery, a journey filled with challenges, breakthroughs, and limitless possibilities. It's about embracing the artistry in code, the elegance in algorithms, and the perseverance in debugging to unlock the full potential of artificial intelligence.

It's through this lens of creativity, problem-solving, and ethical consideration that we can truly harness the potential of AI, programming not just machines but a future where technology and humanity converge in harmony.

PROGRAMMING LANGUAGES IN AI

Programming languages and AI technology are intricately intertwined, forming the very basis of AI. Humans use these languages to communicate complex instructions, algorithms, and data-processing tasks to machines. The essence of AI development lies in the creation of algorithms that can learn from and make decisions based on data. This requires a programming environment that is both flexible and powerful enough to handle intricate computations, data analysis, and machine learning (ML) processes. The choice of programming language can significantly affect the efficiency, scalability, and success of an AI project.

Programming languages in AI are not just tools but also enablers of innovation and creativity. Developers can use them to create algorithms that imitate cognitive functions like learning, problem-solving, and decision-making. This capability is the cornerstone of AI systems, from simple automated responses to complex machine learning and neural network algorithms. The languages used in AI development need to support the seamless integration of various AI libraries and frameworks, facilitating the creation of sophisticated AI models and applications.

The evolution of programming languages has been symbiotic with the advancement of AI technologies. As AI research pushes the boundaries of what's possible, programming languages evolve to accommodate new methodologies and techniques. This dynamic relationship underscores the critical role of programming languages in the ongoing development and expansion of AI capabilities.

Leading Programming Languages

In the realm of AI development, several programming languages stand out for their features, community support, and adaptability to AI-specific tasks. Below, we explore some of the leading programming languages that are shaping the future of AI.

Python

Widely recognized for its simplicity and readability, Python has become the go-to language for AI and machine learning projects. Its extensive selection of libraries and frameworks, such as TensorFlow, Keras, and PyTorch, simplifies the development of complex AI algorithms. Python's versatility allows developers to implement a wide range of AI applications, from natural language processing (NLP) to deep learning models, with relative ease and efficiency.

Java

Java's platform independence, ease of debugging, and the ability to write once and run anywhere (WORA) make it a preferred choice for developing scalable AI applications. Its robustness and object-oriented design facilitate the creation of large-scale, enterprise-level AI systems. Java's libraries, such as Deeplearning4j, allow for sophisticated AI implementations, including neural networks and real-time data analysis applications.

C++

For AI projects requiring high performance and efficiency, C++ is often the preferred language. It offers faster execution times and a lower-level system access, which can be crucial for real-time AI applications and complex simulations. While it may have a steeper learning curve, the control and efficiency C++ provides are unmatched, making it ideal for performance-critical AI applications.

JavaScript

JavaScript's role in AI development has grown, particularly in the context of web-based applications. Libraries like TensorFlow.js allow developers to run AI models directly in the browser, making AI more accessible to end-users. JavaScript's ability to integrate AI functionalities into web applications opens up possibilities for interactive, AI-driven websites and applications.

Julia

Julia is designed to address the need for high-performance numerical and computational analysis, making it particularly well-suited for AI applications involving complex mathematical calculations. Its ability to compile high-performance code and its efficient handling of concurrent, parallel, and distributed computing are significant advantages in AI and machine learning projects.

LISP

As one of the oldest programming languages, LISP holds a special place in AI history. Its unique features, such as symbolic expression processing and dynamic typing, have made it a preferred choice for early AI research. Though less popular now, LISP's influence on AI programming paradigms and its use in specialized AI applications cannot be understated.

Haskell, Scala, R, Prolog

Other languages like Haskell, Scala, R, and Prolog each contribute uniquely to AI development. Haskell offers a strong type system and pure functional programming capabilities. Scala allows for scalable and complex system development. R is favored for statistical analysis and data visualization, which is crucial for data-driven AI models. Prolog, designed for logic programming, excels in AI tasks that involve rule-based logical queries.

Each of these languages has its strengths and niches within the AI development landscape. The choice of programming language often depends on the specific requirements of the AI project, including performance needs, scalability, and the type of AI application being developed. Understanding the features and capabilities of these languages is crucial for developers looking to harness the full potential of AI technologies.

UNVEILING THE POWER OF AI FRAMEWORKS AND LIBRARIES

Embarking on an AI project is like setting out on a grand adventure in the realm of technology. The programming languages you choose are your basic tools—your compass and map. But to navigate the complex terrain of artificial intelligence, you need more than just tools; you need the right gear. This is where AI frameworks and libraries come into play, acting as your indispensable gear, making the journey not only possible but also exhilarating.

The Essence of AI Frameworks

Imagine trying to build a skyscraper from scratch with nothing but your bare hands. Daunting, isn't it? This is akin to developing AI applications without the aid of frameworks and libraries. AI frameworks are the cranes and scaffolding that lift your project from the ground up, providing a structure to support your aspirations. They encapsulate complex algorithms into user-friendly interfaces, letting you stand on the shoulders of giants. The true magic lies not just in their ability to simplify AI development but in their power to inspire innovation by making what once seemed complex and inaccessible straightforward and achievable.

Selecting the perfect AI framework is akin to choosing the right gear for an expedition. Performance is your durability —essential for the long haul. Community support acts as your guide, offering wisdom and assistance when you face the unknown. Flexibility is your versatility, allowing you to adapt to changing conditions. Last, ease of learning ensures that you can use your gear effectively without unnecessary struggle. Together, these factors ensure that your journey into AI development is not only successful but also enjoyable.

Navigating AI Frameworks

Let's delve into the specifics of some trailblazers in the world of AI frameworks, each with its own unique strengths and domains of application.

- **TensorFlow:** Imagine a toolkit so versatile that it can mold to any shape of AI you wish to create. TensorFlow, with its roots in Google's vast ecosystem, offers just that. Its broad acceptance and scalability make it akin to a Swiss Army knife for AI developers (Melnik, 2023).
- **Keras:** Think of Keras as your best friend in the AI development journey—approachable, easy to get along with, and always there to simplify things for you. It democratizes deep learning, making the power of neural networks accessible to all (Evans, 2023).
- **PyTorch:** PyTorch, with its dynamic computation graphs, is like having a magic wand that lets your AI models morph and adapt as you experiment. It's the playground of academia, where the boundaries of AI are pushed daily (Melnik, 2023).
- **Scikit-learn:** For those times when you need to get back to basics, Scikit-learn is there. It's the trusty compass that guides you through the world of classical machine learning, reliable and straightforward (Melnik, 2023).
- **Microsoft Cognitive Toolkit (CNTK):** Imagine a framework that scales with your ambitions, growing in power as your data grows. The Microsoft Cognitive Toolkit is a scalable partner ready to tackle the most demanding AI challenges.
- **DL4J (Deeplearning4j):** For the adventurers who have chosen the path of Java, DL4J is your shield and sword, integrating AI into the Java ecosystem with grace and efficiency. It's the bridge between the

worlds of big data and AI, enabling powerful, distributed computing (Evans, 2023).

Each of these frameworks offers a unique set of capabilities designed to empower developers to bring their AI visions to life. Whether you're crafting intricate neural networks, analyzing vast datasets, or automating intelligent behaviors, there's a framework tailored to your needs.

In the journey of AI development, the frameworks and libraries you choose are more than just tools; they are your companions, guiding you through the complexities of artificial intelligence. They empower you to explore new horizons, push boundaries, and create technologies that were once the realm of science fiction. So, as you embark on your next AI project, remember that the right framework can make all the difference, turning daunting challenges into thrilling achievements.

THE SOUL OF AI: A JOURNEY THROUGH ALGORITHMS

Algorithms act as the guiding stars, leading us toward the realization of AI's full potential. These algorithms are more than mere strings of code; they embody the very essence of AI, enabling machines to mimic and sometimes surpass human-like learning and decision-making. Let's embark on a personal journey to demystify these algorithms, uncovering their types, workings, and the transformative impact they have on our lives and society.

The Heartbeat of AI: Unraveling Algorithms

Imagine standing at the dawn of a new era, where machines can learn from experiences, adapt to new information, and make decisions with minimal human intervention. This is not the plot of a science fiction novel; it's the reality AI algorithms are creating today. At their core, AI algorithms are the set of rules that instruct machines on how to interpret data, learn from it, and make predictions or decisions based on that learning. They are the architects of machine intelligence, crafting paths through the dense forests of data that envelop our digital world.

The magic of these algorithms lies in their ability to evolve. Unlike static computer programs of the past, AI algorithms adapt and improve as they digest more data. This dynamic learning process is akin to nurturing a garden; with the right care and conditions, it blossoms, bearing fruits that were once deemed impossible to grow.

Navigating the Labyrinth: The Types of AI Algorithms

Our exploration takes us through the labyrinth of AI algorithms, each path revealing different treasures of knowledge and application.

Supervised Learning: The Guided Path

Think of supervised learning as a journey with a map, where the destination (output) is known for each leg of the journey (input). It's like teaching a child to recognize colors by showing them objects and naming the color—over time; the child learns to associate the visual input with the correct color name. In the digital realm, supervised learning algorithms excel in tasks where the relationship between input data and the desired output is clear and well-defined, such as in image classification and speech recognition (*Artificial Intelligence (AI) Algorithms: A Complete Overview*, n.d.).

Unsupervised Learning: The Explorer's Quest

In contrast, unsupervised learning is an adventure into the unknown without a map or clear end goal. It's about uncovering hidden patterns and structures within data, much like an archaeologist discovers civilizations beneath the earth without knowing what they will find. These algorithms are masters of clustering and association, finding relationships and groupings within data that were previously unseen.

Reinforcement Learning: The Odyssey of Trial and Error

Imagine a navigator exploring uncharted seas, learning from each storm and calm, adjusting their course to reach the promised land. This is the essence of reinforcement learning, where algorithms learn optimal actions through trial and error, are rewarded for successes, and penalized for mistakes. It's the science behind the AI that masters complex games and the autonomy in self-driving cars, charting paths through dynamic environments toward a defined objective (*Artificial Intelligence Algorithms: All You Need to Know*, 2019).

Deep Learning: The Deep Dive into Neural Mysteries

Lastly, we plunge into the depths of deep learning, a subset of machine learning inspired by the human brain's structure and function. These neural networks, with their layers of interconnected nodes, are capable of learning from vast amounts of data, recognizing patterns too complex for human or traditional machine analysis. From deciphering the content of images to understanding human speech, deep learning algorithms are at the forefront of AI's most groundbreaking applications (Tabsharani, 2023).

TRANSFORMING THE WORLD, ONE ALGORITHM AT A TIME

The journey through AI algorithms reveals a landscape where technology meets imagination. These algorithms drive the digital assistants that organize our lives, the recommendation engines that know our tastes better than we do, and the medical diagnostics that spot diseases before they spread. They are redefining what machines can do, pushing the boundaries of human potential, and reshaping our future.

As we gaze into this horizon, it's clear that our exploration of AI algorithms is not just an academic pursuit; it's a personal journey into the heart of what makes us human—our ability to learn, adapt, and evolve. By understanding and harnessing these algorithms, we not only unlock the mysteries of artificial intelligence but also open the door to endless possibilities for innovation and progress.

Embarking on Your Python Programming Journey

Welcome to the interactive segment of our exploration into AI development with Python. Python isn't just a programming language; it's a gateway to unlocking the mysteries of artificial intelligence, machine learning, and data science. This guide is designed to take you from the very basics of setting up Python on your system to writing your first program and beyond. Let's start this journey together, step by step, into the world of Python programming.

Laying the Groundwork: Installing Python

Step 1: Installation

Before diving into the code, the first essential step is ensuring Python is installed on your computer. The beauty of Python begins with its installation process:

- **Visit the Official Python Website**: Start by navigating to python.org, where you'll find the Downloads section. The website is intuitive, automatically suggesting the latest Python version suitable for your operating system, whether you're on Windows, MacOS, or Linux/UNIX.
- **Download and Install Python:** Select the download link tailored to your OS. During the installation on Windows, an important note is to tick the box labeled "Add Python 3.x to PATH" before finalizing the installation with the "Install Now" button. This crucial step ensures that Python is accessible from your command line or terminal, integrating seamlessly into your system.
- **Verify the Installation:** To confirm that Python has been successfully installed, open your command line (cmd) or terminal on MacOS/Linux. Enter the command python --version and press Enter. If the installation was successful, you should see the

installed version of Python displayed, signaling that Python is ready for your commands.

Embracing the Basics

Step 2: Fundamental Concepts

Python is celebrated for its clear syntax and readability, making it an ideal starting point for beginners. As you step into this new world, here are some foundational concepts to familiarize yourself with:

- **Variables and Data Types:** Variables in Python can be imagined as containers holding data values. Unlike some languages that require explicit declarations, Python variables come into existence the moment you assign them a value. The language supports various data types, such as integers (int), floating-point numbers (float), strings (str), and booleans (bool), each serving different data manipulation needs.
- **Operators:** Python utilizes symbols to conduct operations on variables and values. Operators are categorized into groups such as arithmetic (+, -, *, /), assignment (=, +=, -=), comparison (==, !=, >, <), and logical (and, or, not) operators, facilitating a broad range of mathematical and logical operations.
- **Control Flow:** The control flow mechanisms, including if, elif, and else statements, introduce decision-making into your programs, allowing the execution of specific blocks of code based on certain conditions.

Exploring Python's Interactive Mode

Step 3: Python as a Calculator

Python's interactive mode provides a sandbox for immediate feedback and experimentation:

- Open your command line or terminal and type Python to enter the interactive mode.
- Experiment with basic operations. Input 2 + 3 and press Enter to see Python perform arithmetic calculations in real time.
- Test various operations like subtraction (-), multiplication (*), division (/), and exponentiation (**), and use parentheses to organize operations, exemplifying Python's versatility as a calculator.

Crafting Your First Python Script

Step 4: The "Hello, Python World!" Program

The tradition of beginning with a "Hello, Python World!" program is a meaningful initiation into coding:

- **Create the Script:** Open a text editor (Notepad, TextEdit, Gedit) or an IDE (VSCode, PyCharm) and enter print("Hello, Python World!"). This simple line instructs Python to display the phrase "Hello, Python World!".
- **Save and Execute:** Save your script with a .py extension, such as hello_pythonworld.py. Navigate to the script's directory in your command line or terminal, execute it by typing python

hello_pythonworld.py, and witness the birth of your first Python program.

Diving Deeper: Advanced Python Concepts

Step 5: Broadening Your Python Horizons

With the basics under your belt, you're now ready to explore Python's vast ecosystem:

- **Data Analysis with Pandas:** Dive into Pandas, a powerful library for data manipulation and analysis. Start by loading a dataset into a DataFrame and use Pandas to explore and manipulate the data.
- **Web Scraping with Beautiful Soup:** Beautiful Soup simplifies the task of parsing HTML and XML documents, making it an essential tool for web scraping. Practice extracting data from web pages and learn how to navigate and manipulate the extracted information.
- **Machine Learning with Scikit-learn:** Scikit-learn offers accessible tools for data mining and analysis. Begin with simple machine learning tasks, such as fitting a model to a dataset and making predictions. Explore various algorithms and discover how they can be applied to solve real-world problems.

Remember, the journey of learning Python is ongoing. The more you practice and experiment, the more proficient you'll become. Engage with the community, contribute to projects, and never hesitate to seek help from the myriad of resources available online.

The skills you've begun to develop and the concepts you've explored serve as foundational stones for the next chapter of your journey in AI development. Python, with its simplicity, versatility, and powerful libraries, is your ally in translating complex ideas into tangible solutions. The path ahead is filled with opportunities to dive deeper into specialized areas of AI, from crafting sophisticated algorithms that drive machine learning models to harness the power of data to uncover insights and predict trends.

As we transition from the technical mastery of programming languages and tools to the broader implications of AI technology, it's crucial to remember that the power of AI extends beyond code. The upcoming discussions will navigate the philosophical and ethical landscapes that shape the development and application of AI. We'll delve into questions that challenge our understanding of intelligence, ethics, and the impact of AI on society. These reflections are essential, as they guide us in responsibly harnessing AI to enhance human capabilities and address some of the most pressing challenges of our time.

The journey through Python programming is just the beginning. Ahead lies the exploration of how AI, fueled by the code you write and the algorithms you develop, intersects with the human experience. This exploration is not just about what AI can do but about what it should do. As we venture into these discussions, let your newfound skills in be the lens through which you view the potential and responsibilities of AI development. The future is not just to be predicted; it's to be built. With the tools and knowledge at your disposal, you're now part of a community of innovators shaping the future of technology and its role in society.

Let this transition be a moment of reflection on how far you've come and an invitation to dream about where you can go from here. The road ahead is as exciting as it is uncertain, but one thing is clear: the future of AI and our future with it is a canvas awaiting your contribution.

7

PHILOSOPHICAL AND ETHICAL ASPECTS OF AI

> *Harnessing machine learning can be transformational, but for it to be successful, enterprises need leadership from the top. This means understanding that when machine learning changes one part of the business — the product mix, for example — then*

> *other parts must also change. This can include everything from marketing and production to supply chain and even hiring and incentive systems.*
>
> — ERIK BRYNJOLFSSON

AI's influence stretches far beyond the confines of business optimization and efficiency. Its capabilities, from understanding human speech to making complex decisions and recognizing patterns in vast datasets, are reshaping the very fabric of society. This chapter aims to delve into the philosophical and ethical aspects of AI, exploring how this technology is not just a tool for economic growth but a force capable of altering societal norms, ethics, and the human condition itself.

As we embark on this exploration, our goal is to provoke thoughtful consideration of AI's broader implications. It brings forth a plethora of questions and dilemmas: How does AI affect our understanding of privacy, autonomy, and bias? What role does AI play in shaping our social interactions, the employment landscape, and even our global economy? And crucially, how do we navigate the ethical quandaries that arise with the deployment of AI systems in sensitive areas such as healthcare, criminal justice, and personal data analysis?

THE BRIGHT SIDE OF AI IN SOCIETY

Smart technologies have democratized access to information and services, breaking down barriers for individuals with disabilities and connecting global communities in unprecedented ways. Tools that improve accessibility, such as voice-assisted devices and applications designed for those with visual or hearing impairments, empower a level of independence that was previously difficult to achieve. Similarly, the ability for people across the globe to share ideas, collaborate, and forge communities online transcends physical boundaries, creating a tapestry of interconnectedness that enriches our social fabric.

Integrating these smart technologies into our homes and personal devices simplifies many of our routine tasks. From managing our calendars to curating personalized content streams, these advancements free up time and reduce the stress associated with daily logistics, allowing us to focus on what truly matters.

Navigating the Challenges

However, this journey is not without its pitfalls. Privacy emerges as a significant concern, with the collection and analysis of vast amounts of personal data raising questions about security and the potential for misuse. The fine line between personalized services and surveillance becomes increasingly blurred, calling for more stringent safeguards to protect our personal information.

While digital connectivity brings us closer in some ways, it risks diminishing the value of face-to-face interactions, leading to a sense of isolation for some. The convenience of digital assistants and online networks, while beneficial, sometimes replaces the richness of in-person conversations, raising concerns about the long-term implications for our social skills and emotional well-being.

Ethical considerations also come to the forefront, especially as these technologies play a more significant role in critical sectors such as healthcare, law enforcement, and finance. The potential for inherited biases in the data these systems learn from could perpetuate discrimination and unfair practices, highlighting the need for transparent, accountable, and fair technology design and deployment.

Striking a Balance

Blending these smart technologies into the societal structure is defined by its dualistic nature. On one hand, the possibilities for enhancing human capabilities and forging global connections are boundless. On the other, the ethical, privacy, and social implications require us to tread carefully, ensuring that our digital advancements do not come at the cost of our core human values.

As we continue to explore the vast potential of these technologies, it's crucial to engage in open and informed discussions among developers, policymakers, and the public. This dialogue is essential for leveraging the benefits while addressing the challenges through thoughtful regulation, ethical development practices, and public education on the impact of our digital evolution.

Embracing this balanced approach allows us to harness the positive power of technology to improve our lives while vigilantly safeguarding our rights and fostering genuine connections in the digital age.

ETHICAL DILEMMAS EXPLORED

A pressing concern is the potential for AI systems to act in ways that are unjust or discriminatory. Given that these systems learn from existing data, they can inadvertently perpetuate historical biases, making decisions that favor one group over another based on flawed or biased information. This issue is not just theoretical; it has practical implications in areas such as credit scoring, job recruitment, and law enforcement, where biased algorithms can have life-altering consequences.

Privacy concerns, too, are at the forefront of the ethical debate. In an era where personal data is the currency of the digital economy, ensuring the confidentiality and integrity of this information is paramount. Yet, the very nature of AI, which thrives on vast datasets to refine its predictions and recommendations, poses inherent risks to informational privacy. This tension between the benefits of data-driven insights and the right to privacy defines one of the modern era's most significant ethical battlegrounds.

Moreover, autonomy—how much control we cede to these systems in our daily lives and critical societal functions—raises questions about dependency and the potential loss of human oversight. As AI systems become more integrated into decision-making processes, the risk of "automation bias," or the overreliance on automated systems at the expense of human judgment, becomes a genuine concern.

Navigating Ethical Complexity

Addressing these ethical challenges requires more than just technical solutions; it demands a multidisciplinary approach that encompasses philosophical inquiry, legal frameworks, and public policy. Ethical auditing, for instance, offers a way to systematically assess AI systems for potential harms, ensuring they align with societal values and norms. Yet, there are challenges in this process that require transparency in algorithms and a dedication to resolving problems.

Furthermore, the concept of *distributed responsibility* highlights the collective nature of ethical AI development. From the programmers coding these algorithms to the corporations deploying them and the policymakers regulating their use, each stakeholder has a part to play in ensuring these technologies are developed and used responsibly.

Towards Ethical AI

As we consider the impact of AI on employment and the broader economy in subsequent sections, the ethical considerations discussed here provide a critical backdrop. The transformation of the job market, driven by AI and automation, brings its own set of ethical implications, from the displacement of workers to the changing nature of work itself. Understanding the ethical foundations of AI is essential for navigating these changes, ensuring that, as we embrace the efficiencies and innovations brought by AI, we do not lose sight of the values that define us as a society.

In crafting the future of AI, a balanced, ethical approach is not optional; it is necessary. It requires the engagement of all sectors of society—developers, policymakers, and the public—in a dialogue about the kind of world we wish to build with these powerful technologies. By fostering an environment where ethical considerations are at the forefront of AI development and deployment, we can harness the benefits of AI while mitigating its risks, ensuring a future where technology serves humanity's best interests. This dialogue, ever-evolving and complex, lays the groundwork for the responsible stewardship of AI, guiding us toward a future where innovation and ethics go hand in hand.

THE INTERSECTION OF AI AND EMPLOYMENT: NAVIGATING NEW FRONTIERS

As AI redefines the boundaries of what machines can do, it also reshapes the landscape of work, prompting a reevaluation of human roles in an increasingly automated world. This evolution brings to the fore questions about job displacement, the transformation of industries, and the emergence of new skill requirements, underscoring the need for adaptive strategies in the workforce.

The specter of job displacement looms large in conversations about AI. Automation, powered by AI, has the potential to streamline operations across a range of sectors, from manufacturing to services, enhancing efficiency but also raising concerns about the future of jobs traditionally performed by humans. Reports and studies highlight varying degrees of impact, with some roles more susceptible to automation than others. This shift is not just about the loss of jobs but also about the transformation of job nature and the creation of new opportunities in areas where human ingenuity and empathy are irreplaceable.

However, the narrative is not solely one of loss. AI also brings the promise of job creation and the evolution of work. New industries and roles emerge in the wake of AI's advancement, from AI ethics officers to data scientists, reflecting the technology's capacity to generate new avenues for professional growth. AI's role in augmenting human capabilities—by taking over mundane tasks and freeing individuals to engage in more creative and strategic pursuits—highlights its potential to enhance job satisfaction and productivity.

The transformation of human resources and recruitment processes through AI offers a microcosm of these broader employment trends. AI-driven platforms are changing how organizations attract, select, and retain talent, leveraging algorithms to match candidates with roles more efficiently and predictively. Yet, this shift also necessitates a cautious approach to ensure the integrity of the hiring process, guarding against biases encoded in AI systems and maintaining the human touch that is essential to understanding candidates' unique qualities and potential.

Strategies for navigating the changing employment landscape focus heavily on education and lifelong learning as the demand for digital literacy and AI-related skills continues to grow. Both individuals and organizations must prioritize the development of these competencies, not only through formal education but also through on-the-job training and continuous professional development. This will ensure that the workforce remains adaptable and well-equipped to thrive in an AI-enhanced future.

In addition to personal efforts, policy interventions are crucial in facilitating a smooth transition. These interventions can include social safety nets for those affected by automation, as well as incentives for companies that invest in employee retraining. By adopting a multifaceted approach to policy, we can effectively mitigate the challenges and maximize the opportunities presented by AI in the employment sector.

With AI's growing influence in the workforce, the road ahead is filled with uncertainty and opportunity. The journey requires a collaborative effort among stakeholders across the spectrum—educators, policymakers, businesses, and workers—to foster an ecosystem that embraces change, values human contribution, and leverages AI as a tool for empowerment and innovation. In doing so, we can navigate the new frontiers of employment shaped by AI, harnessing its potential to create a future of work that is more dynamic, inclusive, and fulfilling for all.

GOVERNING THE AI REVOLUTION: FRAMEWORKS AND CHALLENGES

As AI becomes increasingly embedded in various sectors of society and industry, the call for comprehensive governance frameworks has never been louder. The swift pace of AI's evolution, alongside its deep societal ramifications, necessitates a regulatory approach that ensures responsible, ethical use while fostering innovation and respecting global diversity in application and impact.

Crafting Frameworks Amidst Challenges

The Imperative for Regulation

Efforts to establish regulatory frameworks for AI are unfolding globally, with the European Union's AI Act standing as a notable initiative. It proposes a risk-based regulatory scheme aimed at ensuring AI systems, especially high-risk ones, are deployed responsibly (Regulatory Framework on AI, 2022). Similarly, regions like the United States, China, Canada, and countries across Asia are actively developing their own approaches, highlighting a universal acknowledgment of the need for governance that balances safeguarding against potential harms with promoting technological advancement (Bower, 2023).

Navigating Regulatory Challenges

The dynamic nature of AI presents a formidable challenge to regulation. Traditional legislative processes often lag behind AI's rapid development, potentially stifling innovation or leaving new risks unmitigated. Furthermore, the complexity of AI's global impact calls for international cooperation to establish universal standards, a task complicated by varying stakeholder interests and priorities. This landscape underscores the need for a collaborative regulatory approach, one that involves diverse voices in shaping frameworks that guide AI toward outcomes beneficial for all of society.

In Practice: AI Governance Across Sectors

Enhancing Public Services with AI

The public sector stands to benefit immensely from AI, from automating administrative tasks to leveraging data analytics for policy development. Initiatives like those highlighted by TechUK illustrate AI's potential to make government services more efficient and decision-making more objective, thereby reducing human biases and promoting fairness (*Case Study: Responsible AI for Government Decision Making*, 2022). Yet, this progress demands robust oversight to ensure ethical standards are met and citizens' rights, especially regarding privacy and data protection, are upheld.

AI's Role in Hollywood's Creative Processes

Transitioning to the entertainment industry, AI's influence on creative processes, particularly in Hollywood, presents a unique governance challenge. Discussions around copyright, creativity, and the balance between human and machine-generated art have come to the fore. A landmark agreement between Hollywood writers and studios on the use of generative AI in scriptwriting exemplifies the industry's approach to governance. It underscores the necessity of balancing AI's creative potential with the protection of intellectual property and the rights of human creators (Nast, 2023).

This governance narrative, spanning from the public sector's service enhancements to Hollywood's creative studios, illustrates the multifaceted nature of AI regulation. It highlights the opportunities AI presents for societal advancement and the nuanced challenges that accompany its integration. The path toward effective AI governance is complex and requires ongoing dialogue, collaboration, and a commitment to ethical principles. By fostering an environment where innovation is ethically guided, and regulatory frameworks reflect a wide array of voices and concerns, we can steer the AI revolution towards outcomes that are not just technologically advanced but also societally beneficial.

CRAFTING A RESPONSIBLE AI POLICY: A UNIFIED APPROACH

In the journey toward integrating AI into organizational frameworks, the development of a comprehensive AI policy stands as a pivotal milestone. This policy not only serves as a blueprint guiding the ethical deployment of AI technologies but also ensures that their application aligns with core values and societal expectations. Borja (2023) breaks down the process of creating a policy that meets ethical and regulatory requirements.

- **A Comprehensive Assessment of AI Applications**

The first step involves a thorough evaluation of how AI technologies are woven into the fabric of the organization. This extends beyond current applications to potential future uses, with a keen eye on identifying areas where AI's impact is most pronounced. Such an assessment lays the groundwork for understanding the scope of AI's influence, pinpointing both opportunities for innovation and zones of ethical and regulatory sensitivity.

- **Establishing Ethical Foundations**

At the heart of a responsible AI policy lies a set of core ethical principles. These principles, including fairness, transparency, and accountability, act as the moral compass guiding AI development and utilization. By clearly articulating these values, organizations can navigate the complex landscape of AI ethics, ensuring that technologies are developed and deployed in a manner that respects human dignity and equity.

- **Governance Structures for Oversight**

Integral to the policy is the establishment of robust governance structures. These frameworks are tasked with overseeing AI projects from inception through deployment, ensuring adherence to the outlined ethical principles and compliance with existing and emerging regulations. This governance mechanism is crucial for maintaining a checks-and-balances system that upholds the policy's integrity over time.

- **Mechanisms for Continuous Oversight**

Beyond initial assessments and governance, the policy must include provisions for ongoing oversight and auditing of AI systems. This continuous evaluation allows for the dynamic addressing of any issues or concerns that arise, ensuring that AI technologies remain aligned with ethical standards and regulatory requirements throughout their lifecycle.

- **Promoting Transparency and Stakeholder Engagement**

A transparent approach to AI initiatives fosters trust and confidence among all stakeholders, including employees, customers, and the broader community. Engagement with these groups provides valuable insights, enriching the policy with diverse perspectives and enhancing its relevance and effectiveness. This open dialogue underscores the commitment to ethical AI deployment, reinforcing the collaborative nature of navigating AI's societal impacts.

As this exploration of AI's philosophical, ethical, and societal dimensions concludes, the criticality of a nuanced understanding of AI's impact crystallizes. Governing AI through thoughtful regulation and ethical frameworks is paramount for leveraging its potential while addressing the inherent challenges. The collective endeavor of AI developers, policymakers, and society in crafting a future where AI serves as a force for good highlights the importance of ongoing education, awareness, and open dialogue.

Moving on to the next chapter, we'll talk about "AI in Investing and Future Prospects." This forthcoming discussion delves into AI's transformative role across industries, spotlighting its capacity to reshape economies and unlock new avenues for innovation and growth.

8

THE HORIZON OF AI: INVESTING, TECHNOLOGY ADVANCEMENTS, AND FUTURE PROSPECTS

As we stand on the cusp of a new era, the potential of AI to redefine the economic landscape is both immense and undeniable. A staggering projection suggests that by 2030, AI could significantly bolster the GDPs of the world's leading economies, with China potentially seeing a gain of 26.1% (Duggal, 2022). AI is not only transforming things but also becoming a popular investment opportunity. It serves as a clarion call to investors, technologists, and policymakers alike, signaling the dawn of an age where AI's influence permeates every facet of our economic, social, and personal lives.

From its nascent stages to its current prominence, AI has transitioned from a futuristic concept to a fundamental driver of innovation and efficiency. This chapter aims to provide a forward-looking perspective on AI, illuminating the pathways through which AI is set to revolutionize industries, redefine work, and potentially reshape global economic structures.

As we embark on this exploration, the goal is to unravel the complexities of AI's current state and future trajectory. By weaving together insights from investment, technological advancements, and speculative futures, this chapter seeks to provide a comprehensive overview of AI's potential to transform our world. It invites readers to consider not just the economic and technological dimensions of AI but also the broader societal implications, fostering a nuanced understanding of AI's role in shaping our collective future.

In doing so, this narrative serves as a guide for navigating the evolving landscape of AI. It offers a lens through which we can envision the opportunities and challenges that lie ahead, encouraging a proactive and informed approach to embracing AI's transformative potential. As we delve deeper into the specifics of AI in investing and technological breakthroughs, we build a foundation for understanding how to leverage AI not just for economic gain but as a catalyst for positive change in our increasingly interconnected world.

NAVIGATING THE INVESTMENT LANDSCAPE

Integrating AI in investment strategies leverages advanced algorithms and machine learning to analyze vast datasets, predict market movements, and identify investment opportunities. These technologies enable investors to make more informed decisions, capitalizing on AI's ability to sift through complexity and unearth actionable insights. In discussing the impact of AI, it's important to consider both the quantitative improvements in investment outcomes and the qualitative enhancement of decision-making processes.

In asset and investment management, AI's advantages are manifold. Automated trading systems powered by AI can execute trades at optimal prices, reducing the cost of transactions and mitigating the impact of market volatility. AI-driven portfolio management tools offer personalized investment solutions, adjusting asset allocations in real time based on changing market conditions and individual investor goals. Risk management models harness AI to better predict and mitigate potential losses, enhancing the resilience of investment portfolios against market downturns.

Practical Steps for Leveraging AI in Investing

Investors looking to leverage AI in their strategies can explore various applications:

- **Stock Piling**: AI algorithms can sift through market data to identify undervalued stocks that offer potential for growth, enabling investors to build a diversified portfolio tailored to their risk tolerance and investment goals (Bowman, 2023).
- **Automated Portfolio Building**: AI-driven platforms offer automated solutions for creating and managing portfolios, taking into account the investor's financial goals and risk preferences to craft optimal investment strategies (Grossman, 2023).
- **Trading and Trade Management**: AI facilitates automated trading, executing buy or sell orders at optimal times based on predictive models, thus capitalizing on market opportunities as they arise (Bowman, 2023).
- **Risk Management**: By analyzing patterns and trends in market data, AI tools can forecast potential downturns, allowing for timely adjustments to investment strategies to mitigate losses.
- **Data Interpretation and Predictions**: AI excels in extracting actionable insights from complex datasets, providing investors with forecasts on market movements, asset performance, and economic indicators.

Steps to Utilize AI in Investing

To effectively harness AI in investing, individuals should consider the following steps :

1. **Understand Your Financial Goals**: Clearly define your investment objectives, whether it's growth, income, preservation of capital, or a combination thereof.
2. **Choose Your Investing Method**: Decide between active or passive investing approaches, considering how AI can enhance each strategy.
3. **Select an Investing Strategy**: Identify the markets or sectors where AI's analytical capabilities can provide a competitive edge, such as technology, healthcare, or finance.
4. **Identify Your Investing Tools**: Explore AI-driven investment platforms and tools that align with your strategy, evaluating their performance history, user interface, and compatibility with your investment approach.
5. **Manage Your Portfolio**: Employ AI tools for ongoing portfolio management, utilizing their predictive capabilities to adapt to market changes and optimize portfolio performance.

The key to success lies in understanding AI's capabilities, aligning them with strategic investment goals, and staying informed about the latest advancements in AI technologies (Grossman, 2023).

The journey into AI-driven investing is one of exploration and adaptation. As technologies evolve, so too do the opportunities for investors to refine their strategies and achieve their financial goals. By staying informed about advancements in AI and embracing its potential, investors can navigate the complexities of modern financial markets with greater confidence and insight.

THE INTERSECTION OF QUANTUM COMPUTING AND AI

The intersection between quantum computing and artificial intelligence is where the future of computation becomes even more intriguing. Quantum computing has the potential to supercharge AI's capabilities, particularly in areas like machine learning and data analysis, where conventional computers are limited by the sheer volume of data and the complexity of algorithms (IBM, 2022). Quantum algorithms could dramatically reduce the time required for training machine learning models, making it feasible to tackle problems that are currently beyond reach because of computational constraints.

The speculative nature of quantum AI lies in its potential to navigate the vast, complex landscapes of data and decision-making processes far more efficiently than current technologies allow. For instance, quantum-enhanced machine learning could lead to more accurate predictions in weather forecasting, revolutionize personalized medicine by analyzing genetic data at scale, and even transform AI's role in cybersecurity through rapid decryption capabilities.

However, the fusion of quantum computing and AI is not without its challenges. Quantum technology is still in its infancy, with significant hurdles to overcome in terms of qubit stability, error rates, and the development of quantum algorithms that can fully leverage this new form of computing. The speculative nature of quantum AI's impact also raises questions about the ethical, security, and privacy implications of such powerful computational tools (Lawton, 2023).

Despite these challenges, the potential for quantum computing to revolutionize AI remains a compelling narrative. As researchers and technologists continue to push the boundaries of what's possible with quantum technology, the coming years may see quantum AI move from speculative theory to practical reality, unlocking new frontiers in artificial intelligence and beyond.

In conclusion, the confluence of quantum computing and AI represents one of the most exciting frontiers in technology today. With the promise of solving some of the world's most complex problems at unprecedented speeds, pursuing quantum AI not only challenges our current computational limits but also invites us to reimagine the future of technology, intelligence, and human potential (Lawton, 2023).

The exploration of quantum computing and its intersection with AI sets the stage for further discussions on other technological advancements shaping the future of AI. As we delve into innovations such as AI chips and neuromorphic computing, the narrative continues to unfold, revealing a landscape rich with potential for discovery, innovation, and transformative impact on society.

AI CHIPS: REVOLUTIONIZING AI PROCESSING

The advancement of Artificial Intelligence (AI) technology is rapidly transforming various sectors, with AI chips playing a pivotal role in this evolution. These specialized processors are engineered specifically for AI tasks, providing the computational power necessary for handling complex algorithms and massive data sets that AI systems require. Unlike general-purpose CPUs, AI chips are designed with a focus on efficiency and speed, making them indispensable for the demanding needs of modern AI applications (GlobalSpec, n.d.; Synopsys, n.d.).

AI chips are a cornerstone of contemporary AI technology, tailor-made to accelerate and optimize AI processes. Their architecture allows for parallel processing, which is crucial for the deep learning and neural networks at the heart of AI. This means they can perform multiple calculations simultaneously, vastly speeding up AI's ability to learn and make decisions (Choi, 2023). This capability not only makes AI applications more responsive but also more energy-efficient, addressing one of the significant challenges in scaling AI technologies.

Why AI Chips Matter

The significance of AI chips lies in their ability to handle specific tasks that AI demands, such as pattern recognition, natural language processing, and predictive analytics. These tasks require rapid, complex computations that traditional CPUs struggle to perform efficiently. AI chips meet this need by offering specialized processing power that can dramatically improve the performance of AI systems, from voice assistants in smartphones to diagnostic tools in healthcare. This specialization is driving a shift toward AI chips in the tech industry as the demand for advanced AI capabilities grows (GlobalSpec, n.d.; Synopsys, n.d.).

The Innovation of IBM's NorthPole AI Chip

A standout example of AI chip innovation is IBM's NorthPole AI chip. This chip represents a leap in AI processing technology, designed to perform low-precision operations crucial for running neural networks efficiently. The NorthPole chip can execute thousands of operations per core per cycle, showcasing an impressive balance between computational power and energy consumption. Its design is optimized for operations that neural networks frequently use, allowing it to process AI tasks with high efficiency and at reduced energy costs. This optimization makes the NorthPole chip a significant advancement in AI chip technology, offering a glimpse into the future of AI processing (*IBM Research's New Northpole AI Chip*, 2021).

Developed over eight years, the NorthPole chip builds on the success of IBM's previous neuromorphic chip, TrueNorth. TrueNorth was known for its energy efficiency, a feature that the NorthPole chip enhances further (Tucker, 2023). This progression highlights the continuous improvement in AI chip technology, with each generation bringing us closer to more powerful and efficient AI systems. The development of chips like NorthPole is crucial for advancing AI technology, enabling more sophisticated applications while managing the energy demands of high-level computations.

AI Chips Over General-Purpose CPUs

The trend towards AI chips over general-purpose CPUs is driven by the specific needs of AI applications. General-purpose CPUs, while versatile, cannot match the efficiency and speed with which AI chips process AI-specific tasks. This efficiency gap is particularly evident in tasks requiring intensive data processing and real-time analytics, which is common in AI applications (*CPU Chips Selection Guide*, n.d.). AI chips, with their parallel processing capabilities and optimized architecture, are better suited to meet these requirements, making them the preferred choice for powering AI applications. This shift underscores the evolving landscape of computing, where specialized hardware is increasingly needed to support the complex demands of AI technologies (*What Is AI Chip Design?*, n.d.).

The Future Powered by AI Chips

Looking ahead, the innovation in AI chip technology, exemplified by developments like IBM's NorthPole, is set to play a central role in the future of AI. By providing the specialized processing capabilities that AI demands, these chips are not just supporting current applications but are also paving the way for new advancements. As AI applications continue to grow in complexity and become more integrated into our daily lives, the development of AI chips will be crucial for realizing AI's full potential. This ongoing innovation in AI chip technology promises to enhance the efficiency, capability, and accessibility of AI systems, driving forward the next generation of AI applications.

AI chips represent a significant technological advancement in the field of artificial intelligence, offering specialized processing capabilities that are crucial for the development and deployment of efficient, powerful AI systems. Innovations like IBM's NorthPole chip illustrate the potential of AI chips to revolutionize AI processing, making advanced AI applications more feasible and energy-efficient. As we continue to explore the capabilities and implications of AI, the advancements in AI chip technology will undoubtedly play a pivotal role in shaping the future of artificial intelligence, heralding a new era of technological progress and application.

THE NEXT WAVE OF TECHNOLOGICAL INNOVATIONS

The future of AI is being intensely studied and speculated upon as we enter an era of unprecedented technological advancements. Experts across the tech industry, academia, and business sectors are converging on a few key predictions about how AI will evolve and shape our world in the coming years.

Technologically, AI is expected to advance beyond its current capabilities, integrating more deeply with other cutting-edge technologies such as quantum computing, IoT (Internet of Things), and blockchain (Bennett, 2024). This integration promises to unlock new potentials for AI, enhancing its processing power, security, and connectivity. Quantum computing, in particular, is poised to provide AI with computational abilities that could solve complex problems currently beyond reach, potentially revolutionizing fields like drug discovery, climate research, and materials science (Bennett, 2024).

Another significant technological trend is the rise of autonomous systems. From self-driving cars to robotic assistants, AI's role in developing fully autonomous systems is anticipated to expand, driven by advancements in machine learning algorithms, sensor technology, and computational power (Mirabella, 2023). These systems will not only transform how we commute and perform daily tasks but also raise important ethical and regulatory questions.

Economic Impacts and Investment Opportunities

Economically, AI is forecasted to be a major growth driver, significantly contributing to global GDP growth as it enhances productivity, streamlines supply chains, and fosters innovation across industries. The adoption of AI in sectors such as healthcare, finance, and manufacturing is expected to yield substantial economic benefits, from cost savings and efficiency gains to new product and service innovations. However, this economic boon comes with challenges, including job displacement and the need for workforce reskilling, underscoring the importance of strategic planning and policy intervention (Duggal, 2022).

Investment in AI is also predicted to surge, with both private and public sectors increasing funding for AI research, startups, and implementation projects. This influx of investment will fuel further innovation, making it crucial for investors to stay informed about AI trends and technologies (Bennett, 2024). As AI continues to evolve, identifying sectors and companies at the forefront of AI research and application will be key to capitalizing on this transformative technology.

Societal Transformations and Ethical Considerations

Societally, AI's impact is expected to be profound, reshaping aspects of daily life, work, and interaction. AI technologies will become more integrated into our lives, enhancing personalized experiences, from entertainment to health monitoring, and facilitating smarter cities with efficient public services and sustainable practices. However, this integration raises significant ethical considerations, including privacy concerns, data governance, and the digital divide. Ensuring equitable access to AI's benefits while protecting individual rights will be a critical challenge for society to address (Van Der Made, 2023).

The ethical development and deployment of AI will continue to be a central focus, with increased emphasis on transparency, accountability, and fairness. As AI systems make more decisions that affect human lives, establishing frameworks for ethical AI use, addressing bias, and ensuring that AI technologies respect human values and rights will be paramount. This will require a collaborative effort among developers, regulators, and users, fostering an AI ecosystem that is not only technologically advanced but also ethically responsible and socially inclusive (Bennett, 2024).

Preparing for the Future

As we look towards the future of AI, it's clear that the path ahead is both exciting and fraught with challenges. The next five years will likely see AI reaching new heights of capability, becoming an even more integral part of our economic fabric and daily existence. To navigate this future effectively, individuals and organizations must stay informed about AI advancements, critically assess the ethical implications of AI technologies, and actively participate in shaping a future where AI enhances human capabilities and societal well-being.

The predictions and insights discussed here provide a glimpse into the potential future shaped by AI. From technological breakthroughs that push the boundaries of what's possible to economic transformations that redefine industries and societal shifts that challenge our norms and values, AI's trajectory will be one of the most defining elements of our future landscape.

ENVISIONING MY FUTURE WITH AI

As we reflect on the rapidly advancing landscape of AI, there's the intersection of anticipation and responsibility. The potential of AI to redefine our world is immense, and understanding how to navigate this evolving terrain is paramount for anyone looking to thrive in the coming years. The journey into AI's potential is not merely about observing its evolution; it involves active engagement, learning, and adaptation. To prepare for the transformative impact, AI is set to have on our lives, careers, and societies; I ponder several questions that guide personal and professional growth in the AI era.

How do I see myself managing or using AI in the next five years?

AI's influence spans various sectors, offering a plethora of opportunities for both personal and professional enhancement. Whether it's leveraging AI for smarter decision-making, enhancing productivity through automation, or exploring new career paths within AI-driven industries, envisioning my role in this AI-infused landscape is the first step toward harnessing its capabilities. I anticipate integrating AI tools into my daily workflow, using AI-driven analytics to make informed decisions, and potentially guiding others in navigating AI applications in our industry.

What steps must I take now to effectively utilize AI in my personal or professional life?

To effectively harness AI, I recognize the importance of education and familiarity with AI concepts, tools, and applications relevant to my field. I plan to enroll in online courses, attend workshops, and participate in AI-related discussions and forums to demystify AI and make it more accessible. Fostering a culture of innovation within my workplace or personal projects can encourage the exploration and implementation of AI solutions. It's about creating an environment where learning and experimentation with AI are not just encouraged but celebrated.

How do I plan to stay informed and updated about advancements in AI technology?

Staying abreast of AI advancements requires a proactive approach. I commit to following reputable AI research publications, technology news outlets, and thought leaders in the AI space on social media. Joining AI-focused professional groups and networks will also provide me with insights into the latest research, trends, and discussions in the field. This continuous engagement with AI resources will be crucial in keeping my knowledge current and applicable.

What potential challenges do I foresee in adapting to the evolving AI landscape, and how do I plan to overcome them?

Navigating AI's evolving landscape may present challenges such as skill gaps, ethical considerations, and the need for new regulatory frameworks. Addressing these challenges involves continuous learning, ethical deliberation, and engagement with policy discussions. Advocating for and taking part in the development of AI literacy programs and ethical guidelines in my community or industry can contribute to a more inclusive and responsible AI future. I also recognize the importance of flexibility and adaptability as key traits in overcoming these challenges.

How do I envision AI impacting my daily life, work, or industry in the next five years?

AI's impact on daily life, work, and industry is expected to be profound, streamlining processes, enabling new services and products, and potentially reshaping job roles and market dynamics. By envisioning this impact, we can identify areas for growth and innovation, prepare for shifts in the job market, and leverage AI for societal benefit. I expect AI to significantly influence data-driven decision-making, automate routine tasks, and open new avenues for creativity and innovation in my field.

Preparing for an AI-Driven Future

As we conclude my exploration of AI's horizon, I hope you are as struck as I am by the dual nature of excitement and responsibility that accompanies this technological evolution. AI, with its transformative potential, is not a force to be feared but an evolution to be understood, embraced, and guided. The insights gathered throughout this journey underscore the critical need for preparedness, ethical engagement, and continuous learning.

Linking the insights from various discussions, it's evident that AI's integration into our lives and societies is multifaceted, touching upon technological advancements, economic opportunities, societal shifts, and ethical considerations. As AI continues to evolve, equipping ourselves with the knowledge and tools necessary to navigate this landscape becomes imperative.

To effectively leverage AI advancements, I, along with my peers and colleagues, must embrace a mindset of lifelong learning, ensuring our skills remain relevant in an AI-driven future. Engaging with AI's ethical dimensions, advocating for technologies that respect human values and rights, and participating in policy and regulatory discussions are crucial steps in shaping a future where AI enhances human capabilities and societal well-being.

By addressing potential challenges and fostering an environment that encourages the responsible exploration and implementation of AI, we can ensure that AI serves as a catalyst for positive change, enhancing our personal and professional lives while safeguarding societal well-being.

The future of AI is not just a narrative written by technological determinism but a story we all have a hand in shaping through informed decisions, ethical practices, and a commitment to leveraging technology for the greater good.

EMBRACING THE FUTURE

AI is here to stay, and it's vital that we keep discussing it and increasing its accessibility. This is your chance to be a part of the conversation.

Simply by sharing your honest opinion of this book and a little about your own experience, you'll show new readers where they can find it and increase their own understanding of this transformative technology.

LEAVE A REVIEW!

Thank you so much for your support. Welcome to the future!

CONCLUSION

As we conclude our journey through the labyrinth of AI, it's essential to pause and reflect on the ground we've covered together. This book has traversed the multifaceted dimensions of AI, from its foundational principles and technological advancements to its profound implications on society, the economy, and the ethical considerations that accompany its deployment. The journey through these pages was designed not merely as an exploration of AI's current state but as a comprehensive guide to understanding its potential and preparing for its future.

The key takeaway from our exploration is clear: AI is not a distant future technology; it is here, reshaping our world in ways both subtle and monumental. It presents a canvas of opportunities for innovation, growth, and enhancement across all facets of personal and professional life. However, with great power comes great responsibility. The advancement of AI demands a balanced approach, one that embraces its potential while navigating the ethical and societal implications with foresight and care.

Congratulations on completing this journey into the world of AI. Your commitment to understanding this pivotal technology speaks volumes about your readiness to engage with the future. You now stand at a vantage point, equipped with knowledge and insights that position you advantageously for the evolving AI landscape. This newfound understanding empowers you to make informed decisions, innovate responsibly, and leverage AI's capabilities to foster growth and positive change.

As you turn the final page of this book, remember that the end of this journey marks the beginning of another. The landscape of AI is dynamic, with technological advancements and ethical debates continuously shaping its trajectory. I encourage you to apply the knowledge you've gained, whether by initiating AI-related projects, furthering your education in this field, or incorporating AI solutions into your personal and professional endeavors. With the foundation laid in these chapters, you are well-prepared to navigate the complexities and opportunities of AI, contributing to its responsible development and innovative application.

However, the journey doesn't end here. Staying abreast of the latest advancements, engaging with ongoing ethical discussions, and participating in the AI community are crucial steps to ensuring that your engagement with AI remains current, informed, and impactful. The world of AI is ever-evolving, and your continued learning and adaptation will be key to harnessing its potential effectively.

The potential for growth and innovation with AI is limitless. As you embark on this next phase of your AI journey, remember that the choices you make and the actions you take can contribute to shaping a future where AI enhances human capabilities, enriches our lives, and addresses the challenges facing our world. The future of AI is not just in the hands of scientists, engineers, and policymakers; it is also in yours. Embrace this opportunity with enthusiasm, creativity, and a commitment to ethical principles.

In closing, I extend my sincerest gratitude for your engagement and effort in exploring the intricate world of AI alongside me. Your journey with AI is just beginning, and the paths you choose to explore hold the promise of discovery, innovation, and transformation. As you move forward, let your curiosity be your guide, your knowledge be your foundation, and your ethical compass direct your way.

I invite you to share your thoughts and reflections on this book with a review. Your feedback not only contributes to the ongoing dialogue about AI but also supports others in their journey to understand and engage with this transformative technology.

Together, let's step into the future with AI, ready to innovate, inspire, and impact. The journey continues, and the best is yet to come.

ABOUT THE AUTHOR

Earl M. Darwing is the author of *The AI Planet Unveiled!*

Earl has worked in the information and technology field for over 30 years. He is a software engineer with a wealth of experience and licenses who develops applications and works with algorithms using Java and Python. He has held significant roles, including CISCO Certified Network Professional, Microsoft Certified Systems Engineer, and Database Systems Engineer. He is also a licensed financial investment analyst with a degree in electronic engineering technology.

Earl's work centers around technology, focusing on artificial intelligence. He aims to bridge the gap between common understanding and AI's incredible potential. His work has not only given him a significant number of certifications but has provided him with a unique insight into the progress of technology as it develops. His experience gives him a thorough understanding of both its applications and how to bridge the gap in understanding others, empowering them to work with AI and reap the benefits it can bring, both at a basic and more advanced level. His writing demystifies the technology and makes it accessible to people of all backgrounds.

Earl is fascinated by the potential of AI and other evolving technologies and spends much of his free time furthering his research and developing his work.

REFERENCES

Agouridis, A. (2023, February 9). *How AI is transforming the world of recruitment.* Jobylon. https://www.jobylon.com/blog/how-ai-is-transforming-the-world-of-recruitment

AI applications and benefits in education sector. (n.d.). Appinventiv. https://appinventiv.com/blog/10-ways-artificial-intelligence-transforming-the-education-industry/amp/

AI in fitness apps? 5 real-life examples. (2021, August 30). Sunvera Software. https://sunverasoftware.com/ai-in-fitness-apps-5-real-life-examples/

Akhtar, K. (2023, July 10). *Council post: How AI and automation are transforming the world.* Forbes. https://www.forbes.com/sites/forbesbusinesscouncil/2023/07/10/how-ai-and-automation-are-transforming-the-world/?sh=2eb15df84006

Akitra. (2023, December 19). *Five latest applications of AI in cybersecurity.* Medium. https://medium.com/@akitrablog/five-latest-applications-of-ai-in-cybersecurity-5efacd566691

Anderson, D. (n.d.). *The role of AI in personal health: Friend or foe?* Corporatewellnessmagazine.com. Retrieved February 7, 2024, from https://www.corporatewellnessmagazine.com/article/the-role-of-ai-in-personal-health-friend-or-foe

Anyoha, R. (2017, August 28). *The history of artificial intelligence.* Science in the News; Harvard University. https://sitn.hms.harvard.edu/flash/2017/history-artificial-intelligence/

Artificial intelligence (AI) algorithms: a complete overview. (n.d.). Tableau. https://www.tableau.com/data-insights/ai/algorithms

Artificial intelligence algorithms: All you need to know. (2019, July 2). Edureka. https://www.edureka.co/blog/artificial-intelligence-algorithms/

Ayyagari, N. (2020, February 27). *The timeline of artificial intelligence - from the 1940s.* Verloop.io. https://verloop.io/blog/the-timeline-of-artificial-intelligence-from-the-1940s/

Banafa, A. (2024, January 8). *10 strategic technological trends shaping the future.* OpenMind. https://www.bbvaopenmind.com/en/technology/innovation/top-ten-strategic-technological-trends-shaping-the-future/

Bank of America. (2023). *Impact of artificial intelligence (AI) on the economy &*

jobs. Bank of America. https://business.bofa.com/en-us/content/economic-impact-of-ai.html

Banoula, M. (2021, May 26). *What is perceptron? A beginners guide for 2023* . Simplilearn. https://www.simplilearn.com/tutorials/deep-learning-tutorial/perceptron#:

Bennett, M. (2023, May 17). *AI regulation: What businesses need to know in 2023.* TechTarget. https://www.techtarget.com/searchenterpriseai/feature/AI-regulation-What-businesses-need-to-know

Bennett, M. (2024, January 25). *The future of AI: What to expect in the next 5 years*. Enterprise AI. https://www.techtarget.com/searchenterpriseai/tip/The-future-of-AI-What-to-expect-in-the-next-5-years#:

Beskos, P. (2023, October 30). *How has artificial intelligence (AI) affected creative professionals?* Lytho. https://www.lytho.com/blog/ai-artificial-intelligence-creative-impact/#:

BMP Technologies. (2023, May 4). *How AI is changing the world and shaping the future of technology*. Linkedin. https://www.linkedin.com/pulse/how-ai-changing-world-shaping-future-technology/

Borja, C. (2023, August 2). *How to write a policy using AI [A step-by-step guide]*. SweetProcess. https://www.sweetprocess.com/how-to-write-a-policy-using-ai/

Bower, C. (2023, October 19). *AI policy and regulatory frameworks take shape in APAC*. BowerGroupAsia. https://bowergroupasia.com/ai-policy-and-regulatory-frameworks-take-shape-in-apac/

Bowman, J. (2023, November 14). *5 AI applications in investing*. The Motley Fool. https://www.fool.com/investing/stock-market/market-sectors/information-technology/ai-stocks/ai-in-investing/

Burgess, J. (2020, September 24). *How has technology affected social interaction?* Sogolytics Blog. https://www.sogolytics.com/blog/how-has-technology-affected-social-interaction/#:

Burnett, K. (2024, January 19). *How to start programming in python: 13 steps (with pictures)*. WikiHow. https://www.wikihow.com/Start-Programming-in-Python

Burns, E. (2022, February). *What is artificial intelligence (AI)? - AI definition and how it works*. SearchEnterpriseAI. https://www.techtarget.com/searchenterpriseai/definition/AI-Artificial-Intelligence#:

Capitol Technology University. (2023, May 30). *The ethical considerations of artificial intelligence*. Capitol Technology University. https://www.captechu.edu/blog/ethical-considerations-of-artificial-intelligence

Case studies on best practices in AI governance . (2021). https://rm.coe.int/session-4-peter-bjorn-larsen/1680a44e5e

Case study: Responsible AI for government decision making. (2022, May 5). TechUK. https://www.techuk.org/resource/case-study-responsible-ai-for-government-decision-making.html

Cho, W. (2023, September 27). *Hollywood's AI compromise: Writers get protection, studios aim for copyright.* The Hollywood Reporter. https://www.hollywoodreporter.com/business/business-news/wga-deal-studios-plan-pursue-copyrights-ai-generated-scripts-1235602466/

Choi, C. Q. (2023, October 23). *IBM debuts brain-inspired chip for speedy, efficient AI.* IEEE Spectrum. https://spectrum.ieee.org/neuromorphic-computing-ibm-northpole

Copeland, B. J. (2019). Artificial intelligence - alan turing and the beginning of AI. In *Encyclopædia Britannica.* https://www.britannica.com/technology/artificial-intelligence/Alan-Turing-and-the-beginning-of-AI

CPU Chips Selection Guide. (n.d.). Global Spec. https://www.globalspec.com/learnmore/semiconductors/microprocessors_microcontrollers/cpu_chips

Duggal, N. (2022, March 23). *Future of artificial intelligence: What tomorrow might look like.* Simplilearn. https://www.simplilearn.com/future-of-artificial-intelligence-article

EU AI act: First regulation on artificial intelligence. (2023, June 8). European Parliament. https://www.europarl.europa.eu/topics/en/article/20230601STO93804/eu-ai-act-first-regulation-on-artificial-intelligence

Eusanio, A. (2019, April 19). *The best quotes about artificial intelligence (AI).* The 360 Blog from Salesforce. https://www.salesforce.com/blog/ai-quotes/

Evans, D. (2023, December 13). *The complete guide to python AI libraries.* Hubspot. https://blog.hubspot.com/website/python-ai-libraries

Fedde, C. (2016, January 26). *How Marvin Minsky revolutionized artificial intelligence.* Christian Science Monitor. https://www.csmonitor.com/Science/2016/0126/How-Marvin-Minsky-revolutionized-artificial-intelligence

Fernandes, A. (2023, March 2). *Why artificial intelligence is so important in today's world.* Linkedin. https://www.linkedin.com/pulse/why-artificial-intelligence-so-important-todays-world-fernandes-/

Future Data Stats. (2023, October 8). *AI in smart homes: A game-changer for the smart home technology market*. Linkedin. https://www.linkedin.com/pulse/ai-smart-homes-game-changer-home-technology-market

Georgiou, M. (2020, December 29). *5 real-world applications of AI in medicine (with examples)*. Imaginovation. https://imaginovation.net/blog/5-real-world-applications-ai-in-medicine-examples/

Ghosh, A. (2023, December 5). *10 best programming languages for AI development in 2024* . Ellow. https://ellow.io/best-programming-languages-for-ai-development/

Goyar, P. (2023, May 19). *The impact of AI on job displacement: Exploring possibilities and implications*. Linkedin. https://www.linkedin.com/pulse/impact-ai-job-displacement-exploring-possibilities-piyush-goyar#:

Grace, D. (2023, October 27). *The role of artificial intelligence in personalized fitness apps*. Linkedin. https://www.linkedin.com/pulse/role-artificial-intelligence-personalized-fitness-apps-daisy-grace#:

Grand View Reseacrh, Inc. (2023, September 14). *Next-Gen living: The future of smart homes powered by AI and automation*. Linkedin. https://www.linkedin.com/pulse/next-gen-living-future-smart-homes-powered-ai-automation#:

Grossman, A. (2023, October 23). *How to use artificial intelligence in your investing in 2023*. Investopedia. https://www.investopedia.com/how-to-use-artificial-intelligence-in-your-investing-7973810

Guest Writer. (2023, October 17). *The integration of AI in smart homes and offices: Creating efficient and personalised eviroments*. The Cable. https://www.thecable.ng/the-integration-of-ai-in-smart-homes-and-offices-creating-efficient-and-personalized-environments

Haslam, N. (2023, December 18). *Overcoming our psychological barriers to embracing AI*. Pursuit. https://pursuit.unimelb.edu.au/articles/overcoming-our-psychological-barriers-to-embracing-ai

Hines, T. (2018, April). *Anatomy of the human brain*. Mayfield Clinic. https://mayfieldclinic.com/pe-anatbrain.htm

How AI is transforming investing. (2023, June 15). BlackRock. https://www.blackrock.com/us/individual/insights/ai-investing

How to get started with python? (2019). Programiz. https://www.programiz.com/python-programming/first-program

Human brain - structure, diagram, parts of human brain. (n.d.). BYJUS. https://byjus.com/biology/human-brain/

IBM. (2022). *What is quantum computing?* IBM. https://www.ibm.com/topics/quantum-computing

IBM. (2023). *What is machine learning?* IBM. https://www.ibm.com/topics/machine-learning

IBM Data and AI Team. (2023, July 6). *AI vs. machine learning vs. deep learning vs. neural networks: What's the difference?* IBM Blog. https://www.ibm.com/blog/ai-vs-machine-learning-vs-deep-learning-vs-neural-networks/

IBM research's new northpole AI chip. (2021, February 9). IBM Research Blog. https://research.ibm.com/blog/northpole-ibm-ai-chip

Immersive technologies for education. (n.d.). 3DBear. https://www.3dbear.io/

InvestGlass. (2023, February 6). *¿Qué países lideran la carrera de la inteligencia artificial?* InvestGlass. https://www.investglass.com/es/which-countries-are-leading-the-ai-race/

Javinpaul. (2023, September 23). *5 best programming languages for artificial intelligence in 2023.* Javarevisited. https://medium.com/javarevisited/5-best-programming-languages-for-artificial-intelligence-in-2023-8ba9eed4d5cc

K, H. (2023, November 2). *How to use AI for working professionals.* Linkedin. https://www.linkedin.com/pulse/how-use-ai-working-professionals-himanshu-kaushik-i4fyf/

Kanade, V. (2022, August 30). *What is machine learning? Understanding types & applications.* Spiceworks. https://www.spiceworks.com/tech/artificial-intelligence/articles/what-is-ml/#:

Karjian, R. (2023, August 16). *The history of artificial intelligence: Complete AI timeline.* TechTarget. https://www.techtarget.com/searchenterpriseai/tip/The-history-of-artificial-intelligence-Complete-AI-timeline

Keary, T. (2024, January 29). *Top 10 countries leading in AI research & technology in 2024* . Techopedia. https://www.techopedia.com/top-10-countries-leading-in-ai-research-technology

Kennedy, B., Tyson, A., & Saks, E. (2023, February 15). *Public awareness of artificial intelligence in everyday activities.* Pew Research Center Science & Society. https://www.pewresearch.org/science/2023/02/15/public-awareness-of-artificial-intelligence-in-everyday-activities/

Khan, S. (2020, April). *AI chips: What they are and why they matter.* Center for Security and Emerging Technology. https://cset.georgetown.edu/publication/ai-chips-what-they-are-and-why-they-matter/

"Knowledge Is Power Quotes." Inspirational Quotes at BrainyQuote. Accessed February 26, 2024. https://www.brainyquote.com/topics/knowledge-is-power-quotes

Lawton, G. (2023, November 1). *The promise of quantum-powered AI.*

TechTarget. https://www.techtarget.com/searchcio/feature/The-promise-of-quantum-powered-AI

Manika. (2023, December 29). *Machine learning case studies with powerful insights*. ProjectPro. https://www.projectpro.io/article/machine-learning-case-studies/855

Marr, B. (2018, July 27). *How is AI used in healthcare - 5 powerful real-world examples that show the latest advances*. Forbes. https://www.forbes.com/sites/bernardmarr/2018/07/27/how-is-ai-used-in-healthcare-5-powerful-real-world-examples-that-show-the-latest-advances/?sh=582e18e25dfb

Maven: 8 best AI platforms you must check today. (2023, July 15). Maven. https://maven.com/articles/best-ai-platforms

McCarthy, C. (n.d.). *AI virtual assistants: Types, benefits, and more*. Dialpad. https://www.dialpad.com/blog/ai-virtual-assistant/

McKinsey & Company. (2023, January 19). *What is chatgpt, DALL-E, and generative AI?* McKinsey & Company. https://www.mckinsey.com/featured-insights/mckinsey-explainers/what-is-generative-ai

Melnik, Y. (2023, September). *The top 16 AI frameworks and libraries: A beginner's guide*. Datacamp. https://www.datacamp.com/blog/top-ai-frameworks-and-libraries

Mirabella, M. (2023, November 11). *Council post: The future of artificial intelligence: Predictions and trends*. Forbes. https://www.forbes.com/sites/forbesagencycouncil/2023/09/11/the-future-of-artificial-intelligence-predictions-and-trends/?sh=b3386de23938

Mittelstadt, B. (2021, December). *Common ethical challenges in AI*. Human Rights and Biomedicine. https://www.coe.int/en/web/bioethics/common-ethical-challenges-in-ai

Morgan, J. (2019, July 9). *How to embrace AI instead of fearing it*. Jacob Morgan. https://medium.com/jacob-morgan/how-to-embrace-ai-instead-of-fearing-it-4c1d9feed6c

Morron, M. (2023, October 26). *The intersection of artificial intelligence and society: A sociological analysis in the technological era*. Linkedin. https://www.linkedin.com/pulse/intersection-artificial-intelligence-society-analysis-miryam-morron-k41qf

Nadeem, R. (2023, April 20). *AI in hiring and evaluating workers: What americans think*. Pew Research Center. https://www.pewresearch.org/internet/2023/04/20/ai-in-hiring-and-evaluating-workers-what-americans-think/#:

Nanni, D. (2023, July 25). *The revival of a forgotten science: Cybernetics for responsible AI*. Medium. https://medium.com/@daniele.nanni/the-revival-of-a-forgotten-science-cybernetics-for-responsible-ai-b63dda27ea84

Nast, C. (2023, September 27). *Hollywood writers reached an AI deal that will rewrite history*. Wired UK. https://www.wired.co.uk/article/us-writers-strike-ai-provisions-precedents

Neural networks vs deep learning - difference between artificial intelligence fields. (n.d.). AWS. Retrieved February 7, 2024, from https://aws.amazon.com/compare/the-difference-between-deep-learning-and-neural-networks/?nc1=h_ls

Nextech3D.ai. (2023, May 11). *The importance of artificial intelligence in today's world*. Nextech3D.ai. https://www.nextechar.com/blog/the-importance-of-artificial-intelligence-in-todays-world

Nguyen, H. (2022, February 23). *35 best coding & programming quotes will inspire you*. TECHVIFY Software. https://techvify-software.com/35-best-coding-programming-quotes/

Nielsen, M. A. (2018). *Neural networks and deep learning*. Neural Networks and Deep Learning; Determination Press. http://neuralnetworksanddeeplearning.com/

Northern Brain Injury Association. (2017). *Brain structure and function*. Northern Brain Injury Association. https://www.nbia.ca/brain-structure-function/

Pal, K. (2023, May 23). *Can quantum computing impact the applications of artificial intelligence?* Techopedia. https://www.techopedia.com/can-quantum-computing-impact-the-applications-of-artificial-intelligence#:

Pazzanese, C. (2020, October 26). *Ethical concerns mount as AI takes bigger decision-making role*. Harvard Gazette; Harvard University. https://news.harvard.edu/gazette/story/2020/10/ethical-concerns-mount-as-ai-takes-bigger-decision-making-role/

Pillar, A. (2021, March 10). *On cybernetics and its influence on AI*. Turning Magazine. https://www.turningmagazine.com/blog/2021/03/10/on-cybernetics-and-its-influence-on-ai/

Probasco, J. (2023, December 8). *Generative AI and its economic impact: What you need to know*. Investopedia. https://www.investopedia.com/economic-impact-of-generative-ai-7976252#:

Regulatory framework on AI. (2022, September 29). European Commission. https://digital-strategy.ec.europa.eu/en/policies/regulatory-framework-ai

Rohovnin, O. (2017, October 9). *Where the future goes: Quotes on artificial intelligence & our takeaways*. Phonexa. https://phonexa.com/blog/10-shocking-and-inspiring-quotes-on-artificial-intelligence/

Sajid, H. (2023a, March 3). *AI in education: 5 practical applications*. V7. https://www.v7labs.com/blog/ai-in-education

Sajid, H. (2023b, April 1). *AI in cybersecurity: 5 crucial applications*. V7. https://www.v7labs.com/blog/ai-in-cybersecurity

Segal, E. (2020, June 2). *AI applications in cybersecurity with real-life examples*. AltexSoft. https://www.altexsoft.com/blog/ai-cybersecurity/

Sen, A. (2023, October 20). *The impact of AI (artificial intelligence) on jobs*. Linkedin. https://www.linkedin.com/pulse/impact-ai-artificial-intelligence-jobs-amitabh-sen#:

SEO.AI's Content Team. (2023, September 18). *AI replacing jobs statistics: The impact on employment in 2023*. Seo.ai. https://seo.ai/blog/ai-replacing-jobs-statistics#:

Shamkina, V. (2023, April 19). *AI in education: 8 use cases, real-life examples, key solutions & implementation*. Itransition. https://www.itransition.com/ai/education

Simplilearn. (2021, February 17). *Top artificial intelligence stats you should know about in 2023*. Simplilearn. https://www.simplilearn.com/artificial-intelligence-stats-article

Spataro, J. (2023, June 28). *3 steps to prepare your culture for AI*. Harvard Business Review. https://hbr.org/2023/06/3-steps-to-prepare-your-culture-for-ai

Srivastava, S. (2023a, July 24). *Role of AI in manufacturing: Use cases and examples*. Appinventiv. https://appinventiv.com/blog/ai-in-manufacturing/

Srivastava, S. (2023b, December 13). *AI transforming media & entertainment: Notable use cases*. Appinventiv. https://appinventiv.com/blog/ai-in-media-and-entertainment/

The state of AI in the creative industry: From watson to whatthefont. (2019, November 15). Monotype. https://www.monotype.com/resources/expertise/ai-creative-industry

Szczepański, M. (2019). Economic impacts of artificial intelligence (AI). In *European Parliament*. European Parliament. https://www.europarl.europa.eu/RegData/etudes/BRIE/2019/637967/EPRS_BRI(2019)637967_EN.pdf

Tabsharani, F. (2023, May 5). *Types of AI algorithms and how they work*. Enterprise AI. https://www.techtarget.com/searchenterpriseai/tip/Types-of-AI-algorithms-and-how-they-work

Takyar, A. (2023, April 25). *Role of AI in media and entertainment industry.* LeewayHertz. https://www.leewayhertz.com/ai-in-media-and-entertainment/

TechTarget Contributor. (2024, January 6). *What is natural language processing (NLP)?* TechTarget. https://www.techtarget.com/searchenterpriseai/video/What-is-natural-language-processing-NLP#:

10 real-world examples of AI in healthcare. (2022, November 24). Philips. https://www.philips.com/a-w/about/news/archive/features/2022/20221124-10-real-world-examples-of-ai-in-healthcare.html

Theodotou, D. M. (2023, August 10). *3 tactics to prepare the workforce to work alongside AI.* ELearning Industry. https://elearningindustry.com/tactics-to-prepare-the-workforce-to-work-alongside-ai

Thomas, T. (2023, February 14). *Artificial intelligence in the creative industries.* Linkedin. https://www.linkedin.com/pulse/artificial-intelligence-creative-industries-tobin-thomas

Top 15 artificial intelligence platforms. (2018, January 15). Pat Research; Bigtexts.com. https://www.predictiveanalyticstoday.com/artificial-intelligence-platforms/

Tucci, L. (2021). *What is machine learning and why is it important?* SearchEnterpriseAI. https://www.techtarget.com/searchenterpriseai/definition/machine-learning-ML

Tucker, P. (2023, October 20). *Microchip breakthrough could reshape future of AI.* GovTech. https://www.govtech.com/artificial-intelligence/microchip-breakthrough-could-reshape-future-of-ai

Use of artificial intelligence (AI) in investment management. (n.d.). Infosys BPM. https://www.infosysbpm.com/blogs/financial-services/artificial-intelligence-an-asset-management-perspective.html

The Upwork Team. (2023, July 7). *How to use AI: A guide for businesses and professionals.* Upwork. https://www.upwork.com/resources/how-to-use-ai

Van Der Made, P. (2023, April 10). *Council post: The future of artificial intelligence.* Forbes. https://www.forbes.com/sites/forbestechcouncil/2023/04/10/the-future-of-artificial-intelligence/?sh=1ca388224ac4

Verma, A. (2019). *How AI is transforming the media & entertainment industry.* Wipro. https://www.wipro.com/holmes/how-ai-is-transforming-the-media-and-entertainment-industry/

Waseem, M. (2023, June 23). *How artificial intelligence is reshaping our society.* Medium. https://medium.com/@muhammadwaseem_38666/how-artificial-intelligence-is-reshaping-our-society-fcc4f2f66b59

West, D., & Allen, J. (2018, April 24). *How artificial intelligence is transforming the world*. Brookings. https://www.brookings.edu/articles/how-artificial-intelligence-is-transforming-the-world/

What is a managed database? (2023). OCI. https://www.oracle.com/ph/artificial-intelligence/what-is-natural-language-processing/#:

What is a neural network? AI and ML guide. (n.d.). AWS. https://aws.amazon.com/what-is/neural-network/?nc1=h_ls

What is AI chip design? (n.d.). Synopsys. https://www.synopsys.com/ai/what-is-ai-chip-design.html#:

What is an AI assistant? (2023, August 30). Juro. https://juro.com/learn/ai-assistant

What is generative AI? (n.d.). NVIDIA. https://www.nvidia.com/en-us/glossary/generative-ai/

What is natural language processing? (n.d.). IBM. https://www.ibm.com/topics/natural-language-processing#:

White, E. (2021, July 7). *Top 6 languages for artificial intelligence - bairesdev*. BairesDev. https://www.bairesdev.com/blog/top-languages-for-ai/

Woodie, A. (2023, July 24). *Quantum computing and AI: A leap forward or a distant dream?* Datanami. https://www.datanami.com/2023/07/24/quantum-computing-and-ai-a-leap-forward-or-a-distant-dream/

Yasar, K. (n.d.). *What is virtual assistant (AI assistant)?* TechTarget. https://www.techtarget.com/searchcustomerexperience/definition/virtual-assistant-AI-assistant#:

Žižiūnas, T. (2022, April 5). *What artificial intelligence is and how does it work for creative industries? (16 examples) - attention insight*. Attention Insight. https://attentioninsight.com/what-artificial-intelligence-is/

Zwolak, J. (2023). Ada Lovelace: The world's first computer programmer who predicted artificial intelligence. *NIST*. https://www.nist.gov/blogs/taking-measure/ada-lovelace-worlds-first-computer-programmer-who-predicted-artificial